M000305096

Rooms to Inspire in the Country

THE INFINITE POSSIBILITIES OF AMERICAN HOUSE DESIGN

Annie Kelly

PHOTOGRAPHY BY TIM STREET-PORTER

RIZZOLI
NEW YORK

Rooms to Inspire in the Country is dedicated
to Thomas Jefferson, who created
a masterpiece in the country:
the historic Virginia estate Monticello.

ACKNOWLEDGMENTS

MOST OF THE HOMEOWNERS in this book are our friends. We would like to thank them for their encouragement and support. Nancy Butkus brought us in to edit the *New York Observer Home* magazine, where many of these houses first appeared. Michael Bruno and Alexander Jakowec from 1stdibs.com introduced us to Ellen Ward Scarborough. Jean Herr at *Cottage Living* magazine led Tim to James Cramer in Virginia. The curators of the Sleeper-McCann House in Beauport, Massachusetts, were very helpful with access to their inspirational and memorable property. In Connecticut, Peggy Rossi took wonderful care of our eighteenth-century house while we were on the road. And thanks should also go to Florence de Dampierre, Martyn Lawrence-Bullard, and Jaya Ibrahim for their help and advice; Mike Kelly for his technical support; Christin Markmann; and Sandy Gilbert, Doug Turshen, and David Huang, who expertly organized all of the disparate pieces of this book.

RIGHT: Old roses fill an antique glass vase from Jennings and Rohn Antiques, on a silver tray in the sitting room at the author's house in Connecticut. They sit on a central ottoman.
FOLLOWING PAGE: Fritz and Dana Rohn hung their four-poster bed with antique textiles. The lift-top Continental painted chest, dating from 1820, comes from their antiques store in Woodbury, Connecticut.

CONTENTS

THE APPEAL OF
COUNTRY LIVING

How happy he, who free from care
The rage of courts, and noise of towns;
Contented breathes his native air,
In his own grounds.
—Alexander Pope, *Solitude: An Ode*

THE EXPERIENCE OF LIVING in the American countryside has changed considerably over the last 150 years. Once, country life was a simple, but physically demanding existence. Shaped by rural isolation, a family's survival depended primarily on farming, tending to livestock and growing crops, and their house had to be both functional and practical. With the emergence of the gentleman farmer in the eighteenth century, however, many country houses became stately and sophisticated, with more rooms for leisure and entertainment.

Andrew Jackson Downing's *The Architecture of Country Houses*, written in 1850, perfectly describes the nineteenth-century attitude toward rural living. To him, urban life was summed up thus: "God made the country and man made the town." A cultivated life in the country was the epitome of human existence. One of the most important rooms in the house was a library where "there must be nooks . . . where one would love to linger; windows, where one can enjoy the quiet landscape leisurely; cosy rooms, where all domestic fireside joys are invited to dwell," he wrote.

Some of the most inspirational American country houses were built in the late nineteenth and early twentieth centuries. Beauport, on the Massachusetts coast, was built in the early twentieth century, and decorated in a very personal way using furniture and decorative objects from both the eighteenth and nineteenth centuries—which has enthralled design enthusiasts for nearly a hundred years. The summer home of decorator Henry Davis Sleeper, Beauport is filled with themed rooms of his own invention. He re-created an Early American kitchen, a sea captain's retreat, and one of my favorite rooms anywhere— the Octagon Room, its dark eggplant-panelled walls enlivened with Sleeper's collection of rare French red tole. In New York, another extraordinary example is Olana, overlooking the Hudson River with views of the Catskill Mountains. The artist Frederic Edwin Church bought the land in 1860, and he spent the next thirty years creating a Moorish fantasy with the help of architect Calvert Vaux. This Hudson River School artist designed stencils and decorated the walls and ceilings in bright Persian-inspired colors.

Country life has always had a hold on our imaginations. Whether we spend our childhood in wide-open spaces or in a New York townhouse, many of us have deep within a strong desire to connect with nature. I grew up in the Australian countryside and spent my childhood riding horses over my family's sheep farm. After many years of living in a city, I longed for more space and the wonderful feeling of being surrounded by land, and so Tim and I bought seven acres in rural Connecticut. Now just a simple walk with the quiet sounds of the forest and fields in the fresh green beauty of the countryside brings childhood memories flooding back and returns me to the world that I had left behind.

Entertaining friends has always been an aspect of rural living at its best. A country house has the space to hold big festive outdoor parties in the summer—in gardens unimaginable in the cramped backyards in town, full of flowers, with sweeping lawns, forest trails, ponds, and grassy meadows, together with the tantalizing possibility of adding further outdoor

PREVIOUS PAGES: Olana, the home of nineteenth-century artist Frederic Edwin Church, overlooks the Hudson River in New York.
RIGHT: In his summer house in Beauport on the Massachusetts coast, decorator Henry Davis Sleeper chose a dark eggplant paint for the walls to show off his collection of French red tole in the Octagon Room.

rooms and pavilions. Indoors, larger rural houses have ample rooms and cozy fireplaces for relaxing, and a variety of places to stretch out and dream. Some of life's richest memories are of enchanted summer afternoons in the country. The radiant beauty of the garden, the crisp smell of freshly mown grass, the evening light streaming across the front of the house—these are all signs of the abundance, peace, and tranquillity of the country life, a created paradise to enjoy with good friends and family.

W E ALL HAVE OUR OWN reasons to escape, to find relief from the hubbub of the city—whether in search of more space, better schools for our children, or a stronger feeling of community. Happily, country living has never been more comfortable. With today's sophisticated media systems, commercial Viking stoves for the kitchen, high-speed Internet, and FedEx delivery at the door, a country house can have every amenity imaginable.

Today, with the recent explosion of available design and decoration and easy access to furniture and building materials, there is no reason to feel restricted to a typical "country-style" house. The home furnishings industry has expanded monumentally, providing a wide range of choices. Martha Stewart was a pioneer of the new modern ruralism. Continually inspired by her country properties, she introduced us to the fantasy of color-matched chickens, and perfectly cleaned-out stables. Thanks to her, we have a constant influx of design ideas, based on an idealized version of country life.

Sleeper's Golden Step Room was named after a ship model. Overlooking the sea, it was planned as a nautical-themed dining room, with green Wedgwood and majolica plates that continue the aqua-green color scheme.

This book presents inspired examples of interiors that illustrate many ways of creating a country home. This may be replicating a comfortable past in a historic way—on the East Coast there are many houses dating from the eighteenth or nineteenth centuries—or combining the old and new creatively: we can be equally inspired by designer and architect Steven Gambrel's historic house in Sag Harbor, which is a perfectly composed combination of twentieth-century furniture and period antiques from all over the world, or Simon Doonan and Jonathan Adler's *Sunset* magazine-inspired Shelter Island A-frame. The legendary decorator Tony Duquette always claimed that the country was essential to his work. In California he could create his fantasy pavilions and sculptural gardens on a large scale impossible in a city as constrained as New York. Duquette was inspired by follies built as decorative accents on the great estates in England and Europe during the late sixteenth and early seventeenth centuries. As far as he was concerned, the possibilities were limitless. We still build follies today, but they are now more functional—providing shelter, a focal point, or destination.

WHETHER IT BE MURIEL Brandolini's colorful Hampton Bays guest house, or Michael Trapp's rustic fantasy in rural Connecticut, the wide range of houses in this book embodies many different and inspiring views of country life. The one common element is creativity—something that we should embrace with open arms.

Clusters of blue spring-flowering iris add color to Jeffrey Morgan's rural garden in Kent, Connecticut.

PART I

EXOTIC INSPIRATIONS

FOR A CREATIVE DESIGNER, land in the country stretches out like a blank canvas, providing a great opportunity to build something special. This may be just a few acres, or miles of open space. Whether it is a view that triggers a Proustian memory of another place, or perhaps an exotic part of the world visited years ago, or even a conscious decision to build a personal fantasy—however your ideas evolve, there is room in the country to dream and create. I hope this chapter will inspire you to take a few risks and design something that will make people smile, amaze them, or take them on a journey somewhere completely unpredictable.

Fantasy structures in a country setting need ample surrounding space to be appreciated in their totality. Where they are placed—in a garden or in wild terrain—helps to communicate what the designer had in mind. The late Tony Duquette had a strong personal design vision that included his landscapes: avenues of trees and bushes formed striking backgrounds to his outdoor sculptures and pavilions. At his Malibu retreat, he took advantage of natural sites, like hilltops, to build follies that commanded views of the landscape and its surroundings.

Publisher Nan McEvoy was influenced by Duquette, who was a personal friend, but she had her own idea of how a pagoda should look. She brought in an architectural team, and did plenty of research before her large exotic pavilion was built. And, today the local lizard depicted on its roof is the emblem of her olive oil company, McEvoy Ranch, which sells at Whole Foods. It has a view of the rest of the Marin County ranch, but adds exoticism to an existing cluster of buildings, rather than dominating the landscape. Muriel Brandolini in her Hampton Bays beach guesthouse used strong modern color, rather than architecture to link the various spaces.

SOMETIMES THE LANDSCAPE inspires the design of the house. Designer Jaya Ibrahim found acres of open land in Java, underneath a volcano. This gave him the space to create an Asian country villa, which incorporated influences from his childhood in Indonesia. Designer Michael Trapp was also lucky in Connecticut (a state not always known for its views), where he found a sweeping vista over the hills of Litchfield County, and reworked an existing house to take advantage of its site. Inspired by the exoticism of Indonesian design, he hung the house with vibrant silk textiles, added a wide wooden Balinese-like deck, and installed oversize windows to take advantage of this dramatic view. Surrounded by nature, he started to bring it inside, and today, Trapp lives in harmony with the trees and woods that completely surround his property.

PREVIOUS PAGES: Tony Duquette built many exotic pavilions and garden structures on Sortilegium, his property in the Malibu hills. RIGHT: The central palm-filled courtyard at Cipicong, designer Jaya Ibrahim's country retreat in Java.

THE SORCERER'S EYE
Tony Duquette's Sortilegium Ranch in Malibu

"SORTILEGIUM" IS COMMONLY described as the act of divination using books. Although this alludes to the magical qualities of designer Tony Duquette's ranch in the Malibu hills, the name is a poignant choice because the whole property burned down in the Green Meadows fire of 1993. Over the forty years that Duquette and his wife, Elizabeth, owned the 150 acres of dry, desert-like terrain in the shadow of Mount Boney, this place of fantasy and imagination became like a piece of sculpture, or a work of "land art."

Sortilegium began as a country retreat for the prolific designer, and grew into a mode of expression for Duquette to exorcise his creative demons. He used anything at hand for its effect. Duquette's work is deeply fashionable today because he was the ultimate recycler. For example, one of his favorite sources for materials was the army-and-navy surplus auctions at Port Hueneme in California's Ventura County. These auctions, as well as years of far-flung travel, provided him with an incredibly diverse range of raw materials, which he used to build small guesthouses, pagodas, and follies all over the gentle slopes of his property. He brought in stained-glass windows from Victorian mansions on Bunker Hill, whole Georgian shop-fronts from Dublin, the bedroom windows from Greta Garbo and John Gilbert's Hollywood hideaway, Chinese and Indonesian house fragments, and carvings shipped from Asia. From the navy, he bought entire helicopter landing pads (they made great screens) and other unexpected metal shapes.

At the entrance to the property stood a commanding and beautiful eighteenth-century wrought-iron gate, along with several gatehouses, dressed up like Thai pagodas. Duquette loved malachite green and found a termite spray of the exact same hue—this became the foundation color of the ranch. He also adored the look of red coral, and he enlisted a team of workers to spray dead tree branches all over the property with bright red paint. These colors, combined with his lush green spiky plantings, created the uneasy feeling of being underwater inside a giant fantasy fish tank landscaped with exotic pavilions.

A central driveway led down to the prow of a hill, with a dramatic view of the valley beyond and Mount Boney above. On either side sat most of the pavilions and small guesthouses, although roads led off at angles to other small buildings, some of which held incredible treasures that were the result of a lifetime of collecting. English Chinese Chippendale furniture jostled with piles of eighteenth-century Venetian chairs, next to plastic pots with "interesting" shapes.

The main house was reached through a path lined with life-sized carved Indian soldiers, which added to the general sense of exoticism. Inside, the cabin had a comfortably rustic Mexican feel, proving that Duquette was also capable of designing interiors of great charm. For forty years, Duquette hosted many memorable events here. Long lines of cars would snake their way up the canyon on Sundays to attend

A pair of imposing horse statues, bought on a shopping expedition to India, guarded the entrance to the part of the Duquette property overlooked by Mount Boney.

his big lunches. Guests were serenaded by mariachi bands, while his workmen served Mexican food.

Photographer Tim Street-Porter recalls his first experiences documenting Sortilegium: "When Tony saw the first ranch pictures, he was prompted, he said, to get a bunch of workers together and 'make a few changes.' Two weeks later he called and wanted me to go and see his improvements. Perhaps I would like to photograph these? This began a ritual that involved a larger and larger crew of workers, who toiled tirelessly around the clock, seven days a week, erecting new pavilions and laying out new swathes of landscaping. And of course calling me to document each new addition, which I was happy to do. Everything he did was exuberant and extraordinary."

Duquette's ever-evolving landscaping was his undoing: he had so many rows of pots and sculptural pieces lining the main driveway into the property that during the final great fire, the firefighters feared that their trucks would be trapped in the inferno if they drove onto the grounds. After it was destroyed, the designer commented sadly, "Even in its last moments each little house and pavilion lighted up in glory and was beautiful, and then they were gone."

Duquette transformed even the water towers into pagodas, using Thai finials (or chofas) and Moroccan panels that he had included in his set design for the film Kismet.

ABOVE: This fantasy pagoda was constructed with recycled materials, including antlers from the Hearst ranch. This was the only structure on Duquette's property to escape the devastating fire nearly intact.
RIGHT: This teahouse was one of Duquette's most accomplished interiors. He used a variety of fabrics to decorate the walls and carved panels from Asia to create a fascinating multilayered effect.
FOLLOWING PAGES: One of many guesthouses, this small building had a comfortable living room anchored by a red Chinese coffee table. Duquette kept to his typical palette of coral, gold, and malachite green, which he felt echoed the colors of the surrounding countryside.

ABOVE: *The living room at Frogmore House, the Duquettes' main ranch house,
was paneled with an old fence that Tony found in an alley in Beverly Hills. Here, they
displayed their collection of Austrian peasant furniture and finds from Mexico.*
RIGHT: *A colonnade, rescued from a mansion in Los Angeles's now-demolished Bunker
Hill district, ran the length of the Horntoad pavilion. The space was decorated with colorful
cushions, rugs, and a chandelier made of antlers from deer at San Simeon.*

A LANDSCAPED INTERIOR

Michael Trapp's Indonesian-inspired Ranch House in Connecticut

EACH YEAR MICHAEL TRAPP vanishes from Connecticut during the chilly winter months. Owner of an antiques shop in West Cornwall, Connecticut, that is famous for its eclectic and elegant objects, he closes the doors at the end of each year and leaves for the winter. He used to live above the shop, a Victorian Greek Revival house overlooking the Housatonic River; its garden filled with salvaged architectural antiques became a must-see for anyone passionate about landscaping. There is a hint of Tony Duquette in his choice of pagodas and small buildings; like Duquette, he can put antique moldings and columns together in a way that evokes a sense of exoticism.

His new house, just fifteen minutes away in Sharon, comes as a surprise, as Trapp has renovated a traditional twentieth-century ranch house, and the mood is definitely Asian. The big draw for Trapp was the jaw-dropping view of the Litchfield Hills, which gives the house a sense of drama. He also liked the freedom to play with this versatile style of architecture; a historic house would have demanded more respect for its structure.

The skillfully designed approach to the house, with steps up from a generous gravel forecourt, is paved with large slate slabs. The house is perched on a rock, overlooking the view, and the surrounding high stone walls incorporate impressive boulders, some left in place where they were found, others carefully repositioned. The scale and proportion of these walls and steps are reminiscent of those of the

hotels near Ubud in Bali, and the broad wooden deck overlooking the view at the rear of the house is furnished with antique Indonesian wooden furniture, continuing the allusion.

Through the main entrance, a pair of French doors opens onto a small entry area that is shared by the kitchen and a small dining room. This space leads to an open living room, where the dramatic landscape is clearly visible through large plate-glass windows. Eighteenth-century French floor tiles bound by squares of dark wood flow throughout most of the house.

Trapp chose a rustic palette of earth colors. In the main living area, a pair of brown wool upholstered sofas flank the stone fireplace. The ceiling has been opened up, and the newly expanded space has been "planted" with birch trees, dead birch trees that is, stripped to their structural essence, with their white trunks acting as punctuation marks in the room. Opposite the fireplace, the designer has created a surreal tableau: a bare citrus tree floats, suspended above a huge white clamshell filled with red coral.

The rest of the house is reached along passages hung with solid, boldly colored Indonesian textiles. The main rooms all share a dramatic view of the hills. An orange-painted dining room is hung with orange and yellow silk, and matching paper lanterns. A long dining table topped with reclaimed marble squares anchors the space, surrounded by antique black Javanese chairs. A sideboard display of a huge

In the living room, a dried orange tree twists above a giant coral-filled shell.
Empty picture frames hung on the wall are a bold graphic device.

ABOVE: The dining room shows a strong Asian influence. Antique black Javanese chairs surround a table made from reclaimed marble slabs. RIGHT: The living room has a view of the Litchfield Hills. Michael Trapp has filled the space with tall bare trees, a design element that visually links the high ceiling with the stone floor.

clamshell and Chinese shipwreck pottery gives the room a pirate-ship atmosphere. At the far end, a large eighteenth-century Dutch linen-press boasts a spectacular headdress of dried branches.

The master bedroom overlooks the main view, where Trapp created the four-poster bed out of reclaimed architectural fragments. The proportions of this space, and everything in it, have been carefully considered—his palette of faded pinks, greens, yellows, and white is especially harmonious. Balance is established by a pair of matching white lamps on either side of the bed. The room is reflected like a painting in a large mirror, casually propped up against the wall. Above the chest of drawers opposite, hangs a Pre-Raphaelite painting of Saint Sebastian—appropriately set in a landscape—next to a large window, which opens onto a meditative view of the rocky, forested hillside. Trapp has totally dispensed with conventional curtains; instead, gauzy silk panels are simply left to hang to the floor, each pinned to the ceiling by a solitary pushpin.

The principal guest bedroom overlooks a rock-filled courtyard. Painted yellow and draped with Asian textiles, an antique four-poster bed hung with red paper lanterns sits at one end of the room like a Chinese bed. A seating alcove in the window, furnished with Asian silk pillows, is situated across from a TV screen that has been discreetly set into the wall.

Throughout the house, Trapp has carefully composed tableaux of antiques and found objects. Skeletons of fish and plants, coral and shells are placed in thoughtful proportion on top of shelves and tabletops, reflecting the landscape designer's deep relationship with the natural world. The renovation of this three thousand-square-foot house took more than three years, and its echoes of Asian influence are quite unexpected in this corner of Connecticut.

Glass-fronted cabinets lining the wall in a small breakfast room next to the kitchen hold books and Trapp's collection of red and white coral and shells. In front of the window he displays clear glass vases and beakers. The eighteenth-century dining chairs work surprisingly well with the modern steel-based table.

THIS PAGE, CLOCKWISE FROM TOP LEFT: In the living room, empty frames masquerade as panelling. The chair is upholstered in gray wool. In the corner of the master bedroom, a small bare tree is placed on a pedestal for a dramatic effect. The master bathroom features a large freestanding tub. Dried flowers hang from the ceiling. An enormous mirror casually leaned against the wall reflects the bed in the master bedroom. RIGHT: The bed in the master bedroom is composed of antique architectural elements. Posts reclaimed from an old house provide a frame, and the mattress is covered with faded red silk. A pair of black Chinese footstools sits at its foot.

AN ORIENTALIST'S RETREAT

Jaya Ibrahim's Cipicong

CIPICONG IS ONE OF MY favorite country houses in the world. Jaya Ibrahim's romantic retreat is an Asian version of a Palladian villa, and he gave the house exquisite proportions, carefully balancing the design elements of each facade. Inspired by a landscape painting he found at auction in London, Ibrahim built this property as a retreat for himself and his partner, John Saunders. Blending inspiration from a variety of sources—Venetian, Moorish, Italian, and Javanese—he has created a comfortably cool, well-ventilated house that could be anywhere in the world.

Born in Indonesia, Ibrahim has an international design business, designing a far-flung range of hotels including the Chedi in Milan, the Leela Palace in India, the Nam Hai in Vietnam, as well as others in Miami and Mexico. The designer is also busy in China, in Beijing's "Summer Palace," where he is working for the luxurious Aman hotels.

At Cipicong, the designer has distilled the best of his ideas. He has designed much of the furniture himself, with the help of the excellent local craftsmen. Ibrahim has been influenced by many cultural sources, and here he chose to layer Dutch Colonial design with elements of the rich Javanese culture of his childhood. He spends as much time here as possible, as it is quite isolated from his work life, and even more difficult to reach by phone. One of the most important elements of a successful retreat is a sense of separation from the rest of the world.

Visitors arrive along a long rustic drive and ascend a series of formal steps to the north-facing main entrance of the house. The first space is a majestic dining room, which opens onto an interior courtyard, deeply exotic, with glass lanterns hung along the surrounding open passageways. The courtyard is lit at night with rows of waxed candles in ceramic pots on the ground, making it a magical place. Throughout the one-story house, Ibrahim has kept the ceilings high, which is a classic way to keep rooms cool in hot climates. A series of smaller rooms opens off the central dining room, creating private spaces for friends and family. Here, along the south facade, breakfast and lunch are served in an outdoor loggia, screened from the morning sun by bamboo blinds.

On the other side of the house is a large library, where Gothic-style windows give a view of the countryside. Here, Ibrahim displays his collections acquired over a lifetime of travelling—books, fabrics, Asian ceramics, and Dutch artifacts—all carefully arranged in perfect compositions, on tabletops and every other available surface. Next door is the master bedroom, where a pair of antique Javanese doors, acting as screens, flanks a Javanese gilded mirror that functions as a headboard. In back of it, Ibrahim floated a panel of fine silk, completing the composition.

Wide verandas encircle the house, except on the east side, where Ibrahim, in the tradition of rural architecture as a folly, has re-created the front facade of a Venetian palazzo. It is reflected in a shallow pool of water that helps cool the house. Speaking from the site of one of his many current projects—the refurbishment of the Amandari hotel in Ubud, Bali—the designer explains that this house is a "tribute to a vanishing Java."

The east elevation of Cipicong has a Venetian-style balcony, which is reflected in the shallow pond Ibrahim designed to help cool the house. Platforms derived from traditional Javanese seating are drawn up by the pool below the balcony.

PREVIOUS PAGES: *Jaya Ibrahim designed the house around
a central courtyard, filled with palms, a pebble floor, and
rows of small scallop-edged pots that hold candles.*
ABOVE: *A bowl of passionfruit sits on the breakfast table.*
RIGHT: *Ibrahim created this back loggia as an outdoor breakfast
room, so he could enjoy the views of the surrounding hills.
A large water pot on a plinth adds a touch of drama to the space.*

ABOVE: Outside Ibrahim's study, a Venetian-style balcony with trefoil arches frames an idyllic view of open fields and the reflecting pool.
RIGHT: From the breakfast loggia you can view the serene sight of local farmers cultivating their fields.

ABOVE: *In the study, celadon pots are grouped
on top of a nineteenth-century Javanese kas.*
RIGHT: *A cabinet filled with a collection of blue Dutch
china rests in front of a carefully composed wall of prints.*

ABOVE: *In a guest bedroom, a collection of inherited Dutch china, Javanese terra-cotta, and items from the Majapahit period are displayed on a side table in front of a Javanese glass painting.*
RIGHT: *A doorway flanked by a pair of spears leads to a small dressing room. The nineteenth-century Javanese cabinet displays a composition of blue china and pottery on top.*

ABOVE: *A collection of antique glass bottles from a Colonial traveling bar decorates a cabinet in the master bedroom.*
RIGHT: *Ibrahim has layered vintage fabrics, Javanese screens, and a gilded mirror to create the illusion of a headboard in the master bedroom. The bed is draped with white antique linens.*

AN ARCADIAN FOLLY

Nan McEvoy's Chinese-inspired Pagoda in Marin County, California

"IT WAS BECAUSE OF THE LITTLE HATS," explains Nan McEvoy, who would look more at home in Edith Wharton's New York drawing room than in this rustic corner of the northern California countryside. "Some elderly friends of my mother had arrived for lunch, and that generation always wore little hats. As it was a very hot day, we realized that we had nowhere for them to sit while they waited for the meal to be served."

A Chinese pagoda was not the obvious answer. But as McEvoy once lived in Asia, she realized this building project would make a wonderful excuse for a tour of traditional Chinese gardens. She was particularly taken with the paving pattern at the "Humble Administrator's House," which she discovered in the city of Suzhou, two hours from Shanghai. Her architect, Michael Booth of the San Francisco firm BAMO, remembers, "We also looked at the Chinese Pavilion at Marble House in Newport, and another famous one in Potsdam. However, the one we built is just an interpretation. For a start, true Chinese pagodas don't have cupolas. A major influence," he adds, "was also the Chinese-style eighteenth-century collapsible garden pavilion at Boughton House in Northamptonshire, England."

Now in her eighties, McEvoy has always been part of the art world, as a journalist, patron, and collector. However, she never forgot the long summers she spent with her brothers on their parent's ranch in Oregon, so she bought this 550-acre farm as a family compound just over fourteen years ago to use as a country escape for her grandchildren. Within an hour or so from San Francisco, and only eight miles from the coast, it was too foggy to grow grapes—the natural choice for a property next door to Napa Valley. With customary disregard for her age, McEvoy flew in olive trees from Italy to start a whole new venture: Marin County's first organic olive oil farm.

After a long drive past picturesquely grazing sheep and the approximately eighteen thousand low olive trees—"clipped so we don't have to use ladders," explains McEvoy—the pavilion becomes visible through tall redwood trees above a substantial Victorian-style main house, designed by architect Marc Appleton. The compound is perched on the bend of a river, which opens naturally into a small lake where a lone swan floats past, its companions lost to predatory bobcats. Entering an open sandstone terrace through a grove of black bamboo, the pagoda becomes a "discovery." Every November, McEvoy hosts a big harvest party which fills all the buildings on the farm, and the pagoda becomes "the place to sit," as Booth puts it.

The building took shape from clay models rather than drawings, because it has such an irregular shape. The unconventional structure took two years before the local contractor got it right. "We wanted to use rustic materials to reflect the farm, so the walls are redwood and the roof is copper," Booth notes. Inside, a few Chinese chairs in the middle suggest dalliance rather than lunch, although McEvoy, a major supporter of the Smithsonian American Art Museum and the National Portrait Gallery in Washington, D.C., recently managed to host forty-eight people here for a museum dinner. "The paved floor is a complicated design of river rock, slate, and terra-cotta," adds Booth. "The building will eventually change color quite naturally, the redwood walls will weather to gray, and the copper roof will become verdigris."

The sloping green hillsides of the McEvoy ranch are glimpsed through the open doors of the pagoda, designed by Michael Booth of BAMO from San Francisco.

ABOVE: *Sculptor Alex Weinstein cast doorhandles in the shape of the lizards that can be found on the ranch. Originally from San Francisco, he used to work at the American Museum of Natural History in New York.*
RIGHT: *The lizards, here decorating the copper roof by Larry Stearns from Vulcan Supply, have even found their way onto the McEvoy olive oil label. New Zealand artist Mark Davidson designed and laid the intricately patterned stone floor.*
FOLLOWING PAGES: *Inside the pagoda, an upward gaze reveals a thicket of Fortuny lamps from Venice hanging from the pitched bead-board ceiling. The copper dragon lamps are also by Stearns.*

HIGH STYLE AT THE BEACH

Muriel and Nuno Brandolini's Colorful Hampton Bays Retreat

MURIEL BRANDOLINI KNOWS what she wants. As a decorator, she has a strong personal vision that is the driving force for all her work. She is passionate about her design work and cares deeply about her clients. The act of creation inspires her, and so she is always moving forward with new ideas, never repeating herself. In this Hampton Bays guesthouse, Brandolini is her own client—here her rooms subtly change from year to year, although the actual framework was finished nearly ten years ago. It is part of the seven-acre property she shares with her husband, Nuno, which stretches to the coast and includes a main house with a view of the water.

The entry to the guesthouse is vivid and eclectic a long bench sits below a row of Chinese felt appliqué landscapes. A bright-green-painted floor flows through into the living room next door and past the stairs to the upstairs bedrooms painted in rainbow hues. Brandolini has an extraordinary color sense, and she has pulled out all the stops here. Bright green is the underlying motif of the living room: doors, the floor, bookcases, and even the ceiling beams are painted a fresh apple green. At the end of the space a set of yellow and chrome dining chairs surround a pedigreed black lacquer dining table from Maison Jansen. The green ceiling unexpectedly raises the low ceiling height in this room, and combined with the green floor, sets the room off like a picture frame.

This house reflects Brandolini's mixed heritage: the bright colors come from her South American side, the hint of Napoleon III from her French ancestry, and her Vietnamese heritage has inspired the Asian motifs throughout, which pull the decorating elements together. Interspersed are references to her husband's Italian family, such as the graceful sepia prints of Venice above the fireplace. Almost every wall is upholstered with fabrics from Brandolini's vivid and colorful fabric line, which makes it a cozy house in the winter.

There are two bedrooms on each floor. Downstairs, one leads off the living room and has its own screened porch. This room has a striking black cast-iron chinoiserie-style bed covered in antique textiles, kept fresh with crisp white pillowcases embroidered with small Vietnamese figures. A large black four-poster bed hung with a bright pink mosquito net, matching the pink and red floral fabric that upholsters the wall, dominates the back bedroom. With customary bravado, Brandolini has painted the floor and wood trim turquoise.

Upstairs, in one guest bedroom, two white plastic lamps flank a purple silk headboard, their shapes relating to its inverse curves. The bright pink floor keeps the dark fabric walls and ceiling from feeling dull. On the opposite wall a portrait of an Indian rajah hangs above a bench embroidered in purple Chinese silk, deepening the exoticism of the room.

A strong element of Brandolini's design is her use of lighting. She treats ceiling lights like sculpture for each room, gathering them in clusters, or to provide scale to a space. In the dressing room, where you would ordinarily expect recessed lighting, Brandolini has hung large bell-shaped glass lamps. All told, this colorful guest house is a jewel box of ideas; it is comfortable as well as exotic, which is both unexpected and inspirational.

This enclosed porch leads off of one of the main bedrooms on the ground floor. Muriel Brandolini has designed comfortable outside seating here with a strong Asian influence. A grouping of lanterns hangs from the wooden ceiling.

ABOVE: The entry passage introduces the bright green floor and patterned walls that flow into the next room. Panels of Chinese felt appliqué landscapes add an Asian theme, while the bright red lamp gives the space a jolt of modern color.
RIGHT: Elegant sepia-toned prints of Venice add interest to the wall above the living room fireplace, reflecting Nuno's Italian heritage. A Chinese screen conceals the open fireplace.

ABOVE: *Inspired by the strong colors of Vietnamese temples of Brandolini's youth, the bright green is the underlying color of the main living space. A nineteenth-century exotic chair is paired with a Victorian slipper chair, both unified by their shades of red.*
RIGHT: *Vivid yellow and chrome chairs provide a vibrant accent to the dining area. The black lacquer table is Jansen.*
FOLLOWING PAGES: *In one of the main bedrooms, six framed leaf arrangements by Ginny hang above a lush red velvet sofa. A black lacquer coffee table gives definition and anchors the room's bright colors.*

LEFT: *A portrait of an Indian rajah gives this upstairs bedroom an exotic atmosphere.*
ABOVE: *This bedroom has a sophisticated mix of strong colors, including the floor, which has been painted a rich pink. To balance the bright hues, two white plastic lamps flank a curved purple headboard.*

ABOVE: The upstairs bathroom, shared by both bedrooms, features two different vivid wall fabrics. This gives the two-part room an added complexity of pattern and design. RIGHT: The striking black cast-iron bed in one of the main bedrooms downstairs is covered with multicolored antique textiles.

PART II

REMEMBRANCE OF THINGS PAST

That translucent alabaster of our memories.
—Marcel Proust

WHY ARE WE DRAWN to romantic old houses? Are we attracted to their proportions, which are often more orderly and balanced than those of today's new buildings? Or is there something about the atmosphere of the past that attracts us? Perhaps it is a mix of both—we are often captivated by the illusion of gracious historicism in our older buildings.

Cities are in a state of constant renewal—the old rapidly gives way to the new—so it is in the country that we frequently discover some of the oldest houses in America. Whether buried down a country lane, or lined up like soldiers in a colonial town, they each tell their own story, which can be read in the walls and floors.

America is fortunate to still have so many eighteenth- and nineteenth-century houses intact, although their existence is precarious because they are poorly protected. Some historic towns have preservation restrictions, but this usually only extends to the exteriors. Thankfully, there are many people who appreciate these disappearing buildings and are happy to devote time and money to their preservation and upkeep. Happily there are many different styles of architecture to choose from. Farmhouses, often built and then expanded for big colonial families, still make attractive family homes, as they are large and well proportioned; while barns, cottages, and gracious country villas are other popular choices, full of charm and character.

FROM THE EIGHTEENTH century, for example, we show our house in Litchfield, Connecticut, dating from 1740; Jeffrey Morgan's restored house on property in Kent that he shares with his partner, decorator Robert Couturier; and two farmhouses owned by antiquarians Fritz and Dana Rohn. A nineteenth-century house follows: a Victorian in Kinderhook, New York, owned by Jock and Ally Spivy. Bringing us up to the twentieth century is Ellen and Chuck Scarborough's Connecticut country house, which is evocative of 1930s Hollywood.

PREVIOUS PAGES: Fritz and Dana Rohn restored this historic eighteenth-century farmhouse in Milton, Connecticut. (It now belongs to their friends Dr. Howard and Fran Kiernan.) RIGHT: The Rohns accented the master bedroom with bright green trim. A green bun-footed bible box dating from the eighteenth century rests on a nineteenth-century Continental painted desk.

COTTAGE COLONIAL

Annie Kelly and Tim Street-Porter's Gambrel-roof Farmhouse in Litchfield County, Connecticut

ABOUT SIX YEARS AGO, we were hunting for an apartment in Paris. I had just finished decorating a beautiful little place for a client on rue Bonaparte and had fallen in love with the look of eighteenth-century France. Ancient beamed ceilings, romantically paned windows, and the proportions of the period could not have made me happier. I searched for a few weeks, in vain, for the right apartment—a difficult task due to an epidemic of "American kitchens," where perfectly proportioned rooms had been opened up to accommodate intrusively modern spaces. I had despaired of finding what I wanted when an American friend reminded me, "You can find the eighteenth century in America, too, you know."

A month later, we were in Litchfield County, Connecticut, looking at the prettiest little eighteenth-century farmhouse I could have imagined. Along with an unexpected seven acres of land and a stream, it had the added advantage of being within two hours of Manhattan. It even had the exposed beams and antique windows that I had loved in Paris.

This well-preserved farmhouse had already undergone the complex restoration all houses of this period need to survive, so we could move right in. However, it was not French, so I had to figure out a way to furnish it in an American way that was true to its history. The house was built around 1740, when America was still a colony of England, and I reasoned that much of the furniture of that date had probably been shipped out to the new country. This meant we could use English furniture: it would be more plentiful than Early American furniture, and with a greater variety of styles to choose from. We started with dark seventeenth-century oak chairs from Yorkshire. Layer upon layer of furniture followed, and I discovered the perfect type of table: eighteenth- and nineteenth-century American drop-leaf tables, which have a modern spareness and are incredibly easy to find. They can be closed up and parked next to the wall to form side or serving tables, or expanded to fit more people for dinner.

I was relieved that no one had "opened up" the house. This usually makes a small house look even smaller, because the size of the interior is evident in one glance. With lots of little rooms, our house seems larger than it really is. The kitchen and bathrooms had been installed in one of my favorite periods in America for these utilitarian rooms: the 1920s and '30s. The fittings are well proportioned and harmonious, and the kitchen just needed an appliance upgrade.

Upstairs, a few rooms had been carved out of the attic in the 1920s. To make a newer room look old, I wallpapered the master bedroom with a period-style English Colefax and Fowler print. Another space was painted with vertical stripes—a trick to make the ceilings seem higher. Downstairs, the oldest room is the front room, with the original front door. This was a difficult space to furnish. In the eighteenth century it was the most important room, where the

In the dining room alcove, peonies from the garden, arrayed in a nineteenth-century American cut-glass jug, overhang antique American Indian pottery.

"best" bed was kept; consequently, the fireplace sat at one end, rather than being centrally placed. This room is now the "grown-up" dining room, as the awkward space fits a dining table perfectly. At night in the candlelight, with a flickering fire in winter, it is easy to feel that you have traveled back in time to a more poetic, kinder age.

We had no intention of adding extra windows or that horror of modern invention, the skylight. A well-lit house is never dark; all you have to do is turn on the electricity. Another way to bring light into a period house is to replace modern windows with eighteenth-century versions. Larger buildings of that period often had enormous windows that can easily be replicated, and which make sense for today's living.

We didn't have a place for lunches in summer, when nothing is nicer than eating in the garden. Ready-made gazebo kits had awkward proportions, and we wanted a taller, more elegant space that would lend character to the garden. We solved the problem with the addition of an outdoor dining pagoda designed by Tim, based on an English design by John Fowler. Its Gothic archways frame the view of the landscape in new and unexpected ways, rather like snapshots. Our builder, Tony Sparks, talked us out of a copper finial—wisely pointing out the ever-present danger of lightning in an exposed country garden—so he built one in wood. We happily discovered that in the summer we can dine here throughout the day—admittedly we eat early in the evening, because after sunset the mosquitoes eat us instead.

We have never regretted our choice of a colonial house. They are worth every penny, as they are built with organic elements, making them in step with the world outside. Thick plaster walls, well-worn wide plank floors, and stone hearths provide a close-to-nature feel that is missing in most new structures.

Lilac blooms in spring at the front entrance of the author's farmhouse. A comfortable white wicker chair provides seating on the front porch.

ABOVE: *This wing of the eighteenth-century house has a Dutch gambrel roof. The dormer windows were added in the nineteenth century.*
RIGHT: *Flowering clematis climbs the post of the front porch, an original—and rare—architectural detail surviving from the eighteenth century. The antique red metal bin under the table holds birdseed for the feeder.*

LEFT: *The authors painted the entry with a soft milk paint. The seventeenth-century English oak gateleg table, bought from Jennings and Rohn in nearby Woodbury, is a useful center table opposite the front door. If necessary, this space can act as another dining room.*
ABOVE: *In a guest bedroom, an antique wooden armoire is flanked by a pair of seventeenth-century Yorkshire chairs with oak pendants. Two pages of a Taschen calendar were framed and hung above the chairs.*

A striped rug from Pottery Barn unifies the main sitting room. Influenced by Tony Duquette, the author kept the color scheme to pink and green—one of his favorite color combinations. A large seventeenth-century English oak chair anchors the room.

LEFT: *The eighteenth-century English sofa in the sitting room was bought at Christie's auction house in New York. It is topped with pillows made with antique fabrics, from Jennings and Rohn. Matching lamps were found in Los Angeles, while the red lampshades are from Target.*
ABOVE: *This silver tray from the Ritz Hotel was found by the author at the local New Milford flea market. It makes a practical choice for the top of the tufted ultrasuede ottoman, providing a spot for drinks and flowers. The decorative white coral is replica.*

ABOVE: *The old fireplace still has its hook for cooking. This was the original winter kitchen, and the side doors hide baking and warming ovens. A row of mid-nineteenth-century Nailsea glass bottles lines the chimneypiece. The late-eighteenth-century portrait above the fireplace is likely English.*
RIGHT: *The front parlor has been turned into a formal dining room. Additional seventeenth-century Yorkshire chairs give the room a period atmosphere.*

In the breakfast room, a gateleg table from the sixteenth
century is surrounded by seventeenth-century English
chairs. A large piece of white cast coral sits in front
on the window. On the right, an eighteenth-century
French tapestry chair, found at Jennings and Rohn,
provides additional seating.

ABOVE: *On the chimneypiece, a delicate piece of lacy coral bridges the gap between an eighteenth-century creamware plate and an early-nineteenth-century Nailsea glass bottle.*
RIGHT: *An eighteenth-century Scandinavian dresser with its original paint displays the authors' collection of eighteenth-century creamware and antique glasses in the breakfast room.*

ABOVE: The upstairs master bedroom is covered with a now-discontinued print of Colefax and Fowler wallpaper. Like much of the house, here the color scheme is kept to a fresh pink and green. The bed curtains are from Pottery Barn, and the bright green pillowcases were bought at Target.
RIGHT: The canopy of the four-poster bed is upholstered with a vintage crewel fabric. The writing case on the desk belonged to the author's grandmother in Australia.

ABOVE: *A decoupage tray on the chimneypiece, from John Derian in New York, adds to the dining room's country spirit. The eighteenth-century fireplace is original to the house.*
CLOCKWISE FROM TOP LEFT: *A zinc finial gives scale to a nineteenth-century English print and side table in the breakfast room. A collection of colored glass vases filled with seasonal garden daffodils brightens up the kitchen window. A variety of finds from the New Milford flea market, including a pair of ostrich eggs and white pudding molds, enliven the library shelves. Antique prints hung on painted green-striped walls decorate a small upstairs sitting room.*

ABOVE: Viewed from the garden pagoda, the wings of the 1740 Colonial farmhouse look like two old houses joined into one. Painted a dark Tudor Brown from Benjamin Moore, the color suits the period of the house.
RIGHT: Photographer Tim Street-Porter designed a garden pagoda based on one from English decorator John Fowler's garden. Its use as a summer dining room has expanded the house and made it more livable. The sloped wood shingle roof and a jaunty finial give the latticework structure a festive air.

HISTORICAL RESTORATION

Jeffrey Morgan's 1743 Colonial in Kent, Connecticut

WHEN JEFFREY MORGAN SPOTTED a small house for sale on a side road near Kent, he knew at first sight there was an old colonial house hidden under the clapboard. Having lived in Litchfield County all of his life, he had grown up surrounded by houses in a similar style, and this property had all the hallmarks of the eighteenth-century rural period once so popular in the area. Startling original photographs, taken when Morgan first bought the property thirty years ago, reveal a very ordinary house buried under the weight of 250 years of additions. "I can't remember the number of dumpsters we filled," reminisces Morgan. The house in the photographs looks nothing like the charming, historic barn-red place that we see today, set into a beautiful cottage-style garden designed with the help of his friend Suzanne Cole.

Morgan, who is a trustee and active member of the Kent Historical Society, stripped the house back and in the process removed the pink Sheetrock from the main room and the layers of walls that hid the bedroom fireplace. "The high-gloss turquoise enamel paint on the old kitchen rafters took a long time to take off—although dental tools were involved," he admits. Records show that the property was built in 1743 as an adjunct to the nearby ironworks. The main room once served as the kitchen, and a huge open fireplace was discovered under a smaller 1815 version. Today, a mid-eighteenth-century brass and iron clock jack hangs over the fireplace, waiting to turn the spit. A rectangular Dutch dining table dating from the 1670s anchors the room, surrounded by six matching eighteenth-century American banister-back dining chairs. In the afternoon, dappled sunlight pours through the western-facing windows, giving the room a tobacco color. At night, candles are brought out, and time seems to slip back a couple hundred years.

This central fireplace also warms the small bedroom on the other side, a cozy room featuring a four-poster bed hung with nineteenth-century Indian palampores, which faces a red-painted, early-eighteenth-century tallboy from Massachusetts. On the wall is a portrait of an Abraham Gibson of Boston, painted around the turn of the nineteenth century by Ethan Allen Greenwood. Morgan has always loved Early American furniture, and the house is filled with a lifetime of collecting.

Some years ago, Morgan joined forces with the French decorator Robert Couturier, who helped add a guesthouse to the small property. Today, the couple lives in a large house designed by Couturier next door, overlooking a lake, and Morgan uses this picturesque little house as a retreat.

The rear of Morgan's 1743 Colonial house was once hidden by a lean-to addition. He stripped it away and replaced the windows with ones more in keeping with the style of the house. A vegetable garden takes advantage of this sheltered, warmer side of the house.

ABOVE: *In the main living room, a crucifix that once belonged to the Couturier family in France hangs above a seventeenth-century court cupboard.*
RIGHT: *In front of the large living room fireplace, Morgan has surrounded a seventeenth-century Dutch table with a rare set of six American dining chairs from the eighteenth century. He has kept the floorboards unvarnished, which is correct for the house's period.*

ABOVE: On the shelves of his American plate cupboard, Morgan displays a collection of early American plates and glasses.
RIGHT: Another plate cupboard in the main living room provides the ideal repository for many of Morgan's antique finds.

Morgan added a brass and iron clock jack dating from the mid-eighteenth century that hangs over the original fireplace in the main living room. The dining chairs are eighteenth-century American.

ABOVE: *In a cozy small bedroom, a four-poster bed hung with colorful nineteenth-century Indian palampores adds a period note to the room.*
RIGHT: *Across from the bed stands an early-eighteenth-century tallboy from Massachusetts, along with a portrait of Abraham Gibson from the same period, painted by Ethan Allen Greenwood.*

IN LOVE WITH HISTORY

Dana and Fritz Rohn's Eighteenth-century Farmhouses in Litchfield County, Connecticut

IN 1736 DANIEL LORD BUILT a farmhouse a few miles from the prosperous town of Litchfield, Connecticut. Many years later—about 260—this well-preserved property was bought by Fritz and Dana Rohn, antiques dealers who have a store, Jennings and Rohn, in nearby Woodbury. They have always loved old houses and have owned several, which they carefully restored before moving on.

Through the years this house retained its old kitchen, a large room dominated by a mammoth fireplace. The previous owners had installed a well-designed upgraded set of cabinets and a sink in one corner. The couple took a deep breath, and moved the entire kitchen to a lean-to at the back of the house, where they redesigned the space with large windows that matched the character of the house. This left them with a spacious family room, which they made even larger by opening up an adjoining space. Here, they added a dining table and chairs, as this couple enjoys cooking for their friends. The large fireplace is now an important, central part of the house, and in the winter the Rohns, along with their two daughters, Phoebe and Chloe, spend most of their time here by the fire. In the summer, they move to a lakeside house on the shores of nearby Lake Mount St. Tom.

There was considerable work still to do in other parts of the house. A priority was to paint the upstairs guest bedroom, which was a vision in purple with an orange wall and lavender ceiling. Now a pretty single bed hung with a collection of antique fabrics sits in a more peaceful beige room. Phoebe and Chloe have taken over this floor, and their bedrooms brim with their personal collections, projects, and trophies.

Fritz replaced the 1930s front door with an eighteenth-century panelled version, which features hand-wrought iron strap hinges, and added an overhead window light. To do this, he had to rework the adjoining walls and restore the bead-board panels on either side. This entryway leads to another sitting room, where Dana uncovered an ancient hand-painted frieze. Here, they restored the fireplace and panelled its surrounding wall.

Their previous house, shown here, is an earlier residence, built about the same time in the eighteenth century. At five thousand square feet, it was spacious for this period, and while several of the same design ideas are repeated in the new, smaller house, to move required some compromises. For example, the bed hangings had to be cut down to fit smaller beds, and the dining and living rooms were combined. While the family misses the extra space and the larger fireplaces of their previous house, as you can see their new house has all the charm of the old.

Of course, for the Rohns decorating is easier than for most people, because they have the inventory of their antiques shop to draw from—although once a piece arrives in the house, it does tend to stay; the couple has an expensive habit of falling in love with their favorite pieces of furniture.

Built-in arched bookshelves in the front living room showcase the Rohn family's collection of shells and other finds. This large room, with its own door, was once a shop.

LEFT: *A series of seventeenth- and eighteenth-century Dutch and English engravings hang on the walls above the fireplace in the entryway.*
ABOVE: *An English oak gateleg table from the eighteenth century is topped by a Delft vase and other ceramics, and a candlestick. It is the ideal shape and size for this room that is close to the front door.*

ABOVE: *In this new house, which they bought to replace their previous home, Fritz replaced the previous 1930s front door with an eighteenth-century version that includes hand-wrought iron strap hinges (seen on the left). The sitting room is visible at the end of the small passage.*
RIGHT: *In the master bedroom, a Chinese ginger jar has been placed inside the green-painted fireplace. A row of seventeenth- and eighteenth-century apothecary jars line the mantelpiece.*

ABOVE: Dana uncovered an original frieze in the sitting room and stripped the walls to reveal the rest of it running around the woodwork. The fireplace and paneling on the right are period reproductions that have been added to restore the authenticity of the house.
RIGHT: The guest bedroom was once painted purple but is now a neutral shade. The bed is made up with a collection of period fabrics. Nineteenth-century Currier and Ives prints enliven the wall.

AN ITALIANATE COUNTRY HOUSE

Ally and Jock Spivy's Victorian in Upstate New York

AT FIRST GLANCE, THE SMALL TOWN of Kinderhook, in upstate New York, looks just about perfect. It is a charmingly intact Dutch settlement that was founded in 1788. Jock and Ally Spivy discovered the town in 1984 and bought Fox Point, an elaborate nineteenth-century Italianate country house, on a quiet road that leads out of town along fields of apple orchards.

They were searching for a bigger house than the one they owned in nearby Putnam County, and while visiting a good friend, the poet John Ashbery, the Spivys stumbled upon this jewel-like Victorian villa. Richard Upjohn, who had remodelled a local house owned by former U.S. president Martin Van Buren, is believed to be the designer and architect. Influenced by the English Regency style, the brick house has porch roofs painted with stripes that resemble awnings and many of the "wedding-cake" details typical of the period, including a roof cupola, which the couple completely rebuilt.

With the help of local architect Kate Johns, most of the house was renovated by 2002. This included restoring the rooms to their original proportions and replacing newer mantels with nineteenth-century versions salvaged from Elmhurst, a nearby Upjohn house. Rather than replacing the original plaster walls, they restored them, avoiding a classic mistake that amateur renovators make with drywall. This kept the texture of the house intact, retaining the period charm of the rooms.

The Spivys decorated the house with a collection of Empire furniture, which includes family heirlooms as well as pieces bought at auction and in nearby Hudson. The American Empire style developed in the nineteenth century, when there was a lot of enthusiasm for historical styles: pattern books and journals disseminated designs inspired by archaeological discoveries in Egypt and ancient Greece, as well as the furniture of the Renaissance and Gothic periods. This translated into the elegant chairs, chests of drawers, sideboards, and sofas we see today. This is probably one of the most undervalued periods of American furniture, and in Fox Point it is used in a spare, modern manner. The quality of both the materials and proportions of this furniture are obvious. The Spivys' Gothic Revival chairs, which have beautiful lines, work well in these rooms.

The main entrance to the house is at the back, through a small landscaped garden. Here, a comfortable entry area leads to the kitchen, which was originally located in the basement. The Spivys resisted the suggestion to create an open kitchen—a popular choice today that often creates an awkward space—as it would have impacted the period restoration of the house. A small breakfast table provides plenty of room for a quick meal.

The formal dining room, hung with Niagara Falls paintings on a rich pink background, manages to be a modern space due to its elegant simplicity. Ally, a critic, art historian, author, and former magazine editor, describes the art on the walls. "In the dining

The formal dining room has warm pink walls. A nineteenth-century American sideboard stands below the Spivys' collection of black-and-white sandpaper paintings.

room we also have a bunch of black-and-white sandpaper paintings, several of which are versions of Thomas Cole's The Course of Empire paintings. Sandpaper paintings are basically charcoal drawings on paper that has been coated with marble dust. They were very popular in the American mid-nineteenth century." She adds, "Certain artists specialized in them, and young ladies were also encouraged to try and make them." From the dining room, a door opens onto a broad porch at the front of the house, which is perfect for summer meals.

A house of this period always had a formal living room, and the Spivys continued the water theme downstairs by hanging a large chromolithograph of Frederic Church's *Third Niagara*. "I suspect Church touched up our picture, as there is some oil paint on it," explains Ally. "We found it in Vermont, where Church is not as revered as he is around the Hudson." The room also has prints of Thomas Cole's The Voyage of Life series (*Childhood*, *Youth*, *Manhood*, and *Old Age*). "The four original paintings are at the Munson-Williams-Proctor Museum in Utica, New York," she adds.

Upstairs, the elegant proportions of the house continue. Long, high-ceilinged passageways lead to the bedrooms, and stairs go up to the restored cupola. These rooms are furnished in the same spare Victorian style as the rest of the house.

Both of the Spivys are very busy—Ally is finishing a biography on the elegant Baron de Meyer (often described as the first fashion photographer), while Jock is a partner in the consulting firm of Baldwin, Bell, Green in New York City. The couple spend much of their time here. "Not only has the house provided a place for three generations, it has given us the ability to be part of a small village community with deep historical roots in American history," explains Ally.

Gaily striped green and white awnings shade Fox Point's back porch. The Spivys added the cupola on top of their nineteenth-century Italianate country house; the original had vanished at some point over the years.

ABOVE: *A large globe lends scale to the ground-floor staircase landing. Against the wall stands one of the Gothic chairs from the Spivys' collection.*
RIGHT: *The upstairs landing holds an elegant arrangement of nineteenth-century furniture. The expansive ceiling height is typical of houses of this period.*

The front porch, overlooking the road into Kinderhook, has become the perfect place for summer lunches. Next to the dining room, it has a linen-draped outdoor table and green majolica plates that match the awnings above.

MOVIE STAR GLAMOUR

Ellen Ward and Chuck Scarborough's Hollywood-style Colonial Revival in Stamford, Connecticut

LIKE THE LEADING LADIES in the Hollywood films that have inspired her, Ellen Ward Scarborough lives a glamorous life. She is tall, blonde, and beautiful, and glides through her home in Connecticut like Loretta Young on a Cecil Beaton stage set. Her dashing co-star, husband Chuck Scarborough, is a famous news anchor (with more than two dozen Emmy awards to his credit), the author of three novels, and an aviator with his own pilot's license.

Born in Chicago, Ellen studied art and architecture in Paris, and comes from a family who loves to travel. When she returned to America, Ellen became a decorator, but then moved on to importing antique furniture from France. She loves the furniture hunt and has opened a by-appointment store called Ellen Ward Scarborough, housed in the old stone outbuildings at the back of their property. Ellen sells mostly through 1stDibs.com, a popular furniture website that deals mainly to professionals.

Inside the main house, the influences of this cosmopolitan antiques dealer are obvious. Ellen loves Dorothy Draper and the classic Hollywood glamour of the 1930s through the '50s, as seen in the Cedric Gibbons film sets for *The Women* and other interior decorating masterpieces like *Top Hat* or *Auntie Mame*. Little of this is obvious, however, on the approach to the house, as the sweeping drive leads up to a classic Colonial Revival house from the 1920s. But once inside, the glamour unfolds. A bold black-and-white checked floor creates a strong first impression, and combined with the delicate celadon-green of the walls, the silks, and period 1930s furniture from France, sets the tone for the rest of the house. A smooth transition to a pale steely blue palette in the main living room keeps the atmosphere light and airy. Here, the room is divided in two by a central table. A large black patent-leather ottoman anchors the space in front of the fireplace.

The sunporch is a triumph of pink and white walls and furniture, kept from being too "pretty" by the original tiled floor. In the summer, the windows open out to the large surrounding garden, giving the room a gazebo-like feel. This space leads to a huge wood-paneled library imported from Bath, England, which holds many of Ellen's treasured books on old Hollywood. Upstairs is the master bedroom, where a 1940s-inspired upholstered sleigh bed overlooks the property's large grounds.

The Scarboroughs use their dining room, with its chic formality and colorful chairs, mainly at lunchtime, since Chuck has to dash off to read the NBC news most evenings. Morning finds the couple in the pink breakfast room looking like Nick and Nora in *The Thin Man* from 1934, with their dog Oliver (rather than the famous Asta) waiting for a walk in the nearby woodlands.

Ellen was lucky to find a house that was built around the same time as her favorite periods of furniture—it all fits together so well. Apart from Hollywood, her decorating influences are French. "The pastel pinks and blues of the Ladurée teashop in Paris inspired the kitchen," she explains. "And visiting Madeleine Castaing's apartment was also a big inspiration." Known for pairing pale fin-de-siècle colors with black, this legendary French decorator was certainly an influence. The Scarborough house is a perfect confection, a return to a glamorous world we wish we could visit again.

This wing of the Scarborough's Colonial Revival house from the 1920s holds a large wood-paneled library imported from Bath, England, by a previous owner of the house.

ABOVE: *The entry foyer is painted a cool minty green. The white plaster sconces were found at Le Onze, in Paris. A large Belgian mirror is flanked by a set of French chairs upholstered in leopard-print fabric.*
RIGHT: *The bold black-and-white checkered floor runs throughout the ground floor. Here, a Tommi Parzinger leather table divides the living room into two seating groups.*

ABOVE: *A black patent leather ottoman sits in front of the living room fireplace, which is flanked by a pair of violin lamps from Grosfeld House.*
RIGHT: *A close-up of an unusual pair of painted clocks in the living room, discovered in a Maine department store. A tarot-card tower from Florida sits on a round table next to the sofa. The whimsical music-note fabric on the pillow is vintage.*

ABOVE: *The Scarboroughs lunch every day in their Regency-style dining room, where the Parisian chairs are upholstered in different-colored fabrics. The Neptune bust in the center of the table is from Lexington Gardens in New York.*
RIGHT: *The sunporch's pink and white accents are tempered by the original blue tiled floor. The chandelier that hangs above was found in a Miami Beach hotel. In the summer, the windows open wide onto the large garden.*

ABOVE: In the kitchen, the unique painted glass ceiling was shipped from a French butcher shop. The pastel hues of the walls echo those of the Ladurée teashop in Paris, and the center worktable came from Lyon.
RIGHT: Ellen's hat collection and a lively screen found at a New York flea market decorate her dressing room. The marble bathtub was imported from Holland.

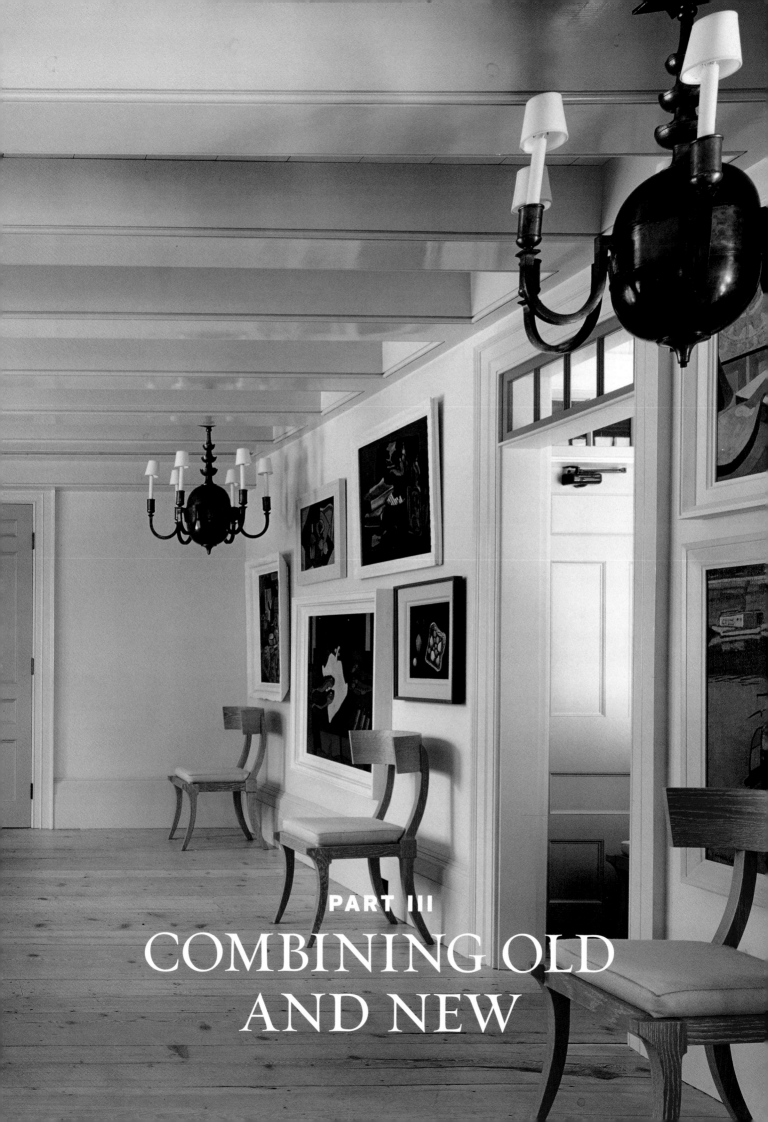

PART III

COMBINING OLD
AND NEW

I T TAKES A CAREFUL HAND to modernize an older house, as you need to understand the original construction and materials. Knowing where the main support walls are is a big help, and provides a guide for changing the proportions of a room harmoniously. A structural engineer once told me that a house is like a ship: each beam forms an integral part of the structure, and if it is changed too much different stresses will cause all sorts of unexpected and unwanted surprises. Many larger older houses need less alteration, since the rooms are usually big enough to work for most purposes; however, smaller spaces may require more thought and planning.

Realtor Chris Cortazzo, with his original Malibu cottages, was lucky because he didn't have to substantially rework his country house. However, decorator Juan Montoya drew on his architecture degree to rebuild his Hudson River Valley property, and in the process constructed a new guesthouse from scratch. James Cramer did extensive work to restore his old country farmhouse in Maryland to reflect its period but also added modern elements, like white plastic Philippe Starck dining chairs. John Smallwood and Carol Bokuniewicz chose to update their early-nineteenth-century Connecticut farmhouse by combining a series of small rooms to create a very modern, airy kitchen with stainless-steel cabinets. Designer Steven Gambrel's architecture degree also came in handy in his renovation; unlike

Montoya, however, he kept to the period theme of his historic Sag Harbor house but added a mix of eclectic furniture to bring the interiors into the twenty-first century.

There is nothing more unsettling than walking into a nice old house and discovering that a new modern glass wing has been attached, limpet-like, to the rear. Molly Duffy and Hugh Burns asked Brandolini to update their late-Victorian beach house in Southampton, and the skillful designer modernized the interiors without destroying the house's character. This is the test of a successful renovation, where there is no sense of separation between the inside of the house and its exterior. Simon Doonan and Jonathan Adler recognized the style of their beach house at once. Built in 1972, they knew that Adler's designs would look great in the funky A-frame interior. As far as they were concerned, the 1970s were "old," and they happily modernized the house with a deck, pool, and a new master bedroom.

A LL OF THE COUNTRY PLACES shown here have strong modern influences, whether just in the shape of an armchair or a whole new room. The key to successfully combining old and new is an understanding of how to blend both styles. With a keen understanding of the original house structure, as well as respect for the indigenous materials, you have the freedom to create personal spaces of your own.

PREVIOUS PAGES: The magnificent main dining room at Steven Gambrel's country house in Sag Harbor becomes a central hall when not in use. In each corner hangs a brass ceiling light from The Hague, Holland, which was found in Miami Beach. The Klismos dining chairs are from Gambrel's furniture line. RIGHT: When he renovated his 1830s Maryland farmhouse, James Cramer discovered old wide-plank floors under the carpeting and rough-hewn log walls under layers of wallpaper. To add a modern look, Cramer bought Marais AC chairs in gunmetal gray from Design Within Reach.

OUT OF AFRICA

Chris Cortazzo's Spanish Colonial-style Cottage in Malibu

CHRIS CORTAZZO HAS LIVED in Malibu all his life, which might explain how he came to own one of the most beautiful rural properties in the area, up a picturesque winding drive into the mountains. Of course, being Malibu's most successful realtor also helps: "I saw it fourteen years ago, when the property was owned by a local family. I probably talked about it on a weekly basis after that—the place got into my blood—so when I heard it might be for sale, I stepped in." This is his second home in the area, a place where he can rest and recharge from his demanding workload.

Surrounded by mountains on all sides, it is hard to imagine Los Angeles is a short drive away. The terrain follows a small canyon, with a stream that becomes a rushing river in the winter but dries to a trickle in the summer. "When you enter the property, you are transported into a different space, because it is a real country estate, with mountain lions, coyotes, foxes, raccoons, skunks, owls, hawks—the bird-watching is amazing!" explains Cortazzo. "My clients can't believe that this exists so close to Los Angeles, as they have to fly to Arizona or Santa Fe for the same lifestyle."

Cortazzo brought in his long-time friend, English decorator Martyn Lawrence-Bullard, to re-create the African ambience that they had enjoyed on numerous safari trips with their mutual friend, musician Elton John. "I went to Africa with them right after I had bought the property, and we got lots of inspiring ideas from the lodges there," he says. Cortazzo was first introduced to the vast continent by photographer Herb Ritts, who was working on his book *Africa*, back in the 1990s, and its immense beauty has never left him.

The original cottage was not large, but Cortazzo didn't feel the need to create a grandiose lodge. Instead, Lawrence-Bullard reworked additional space in some of the smaller surrounding cottages, resulting in a gentler footprint that didn't intrude on the beauty of the landscape. "The setting and main house was beautiful, but the house needed fixing," says Lawrence-Bullard. "We reworked the chimney pieces for a more rustic look, and expanded the master bathroom." Happily, much of the renovation was cosmetic; the main creative mission being to bring an African ambience to the country Spanish-style cottages.

Once past the entrance gates, and driving into Cortazzo's small canyon through lawns that drift down to the small rocky stream, you can't help but notice Lawrence-Bullard's outdoor furniture arrangements, carefully placed in the garden. He takes the concept of "outdoor rooms" to heart here, thanks to new waterproofing technologies. Upholstered living room furniture takes the place of predictable—and often uncomfortable—garden seating. This "Alice-in-Wonderland" effect is like a traditional estate's garden folly, and the lawn becomes a great place to entertain in the mild Californian evenings.

Once inside, the small entry room leads to a large central living room with a raised ceiling, where Lawrence-Bullard has pulled together a strong African colonial look, reinforced by huge photographs of the Nuba tribe taken by Leni Riefenstahl in the 1960s.

The magic of this property touches everyone who visits it. Lawrence-Bullard adds, "Despite the many places worldwide which I have worked on, many of them extraordinary homes, this ranch has become closest to my heart."

Decorator Martyn Lawrence-Bullard built a fireplace in the entry room of Chris Cortazzo's main house and created graphic-looking storage for logs on either side. He designed a pair of comfortable chairs, slip-covered in white linen, to flank an small exotic table from John Rosselli in New York.

Large striking photographs taken by Leni Riefenstahl— her Nuba series from the 1960s—dominate the main living room. Lawrence-Bullard designed the square center coffee table and surrounding furniture, which is upholstered in linen, but brought in the leather chairs to add extra texture to the space.

ABOVE: *A detail of the bathroom shows an antique English shaving mirror surrounded by accessories from Waterworks and apothecary jars from the eighteenth and nineteenth centuries.*
RIGHT: *Lawrence-Bullard constructed the master bathroom out of several smaller rooms and gave it a Carrera marble wainscoat. He designed the étagère and added an Afghanistan tribal rug to continue the theme. The photograph beyond the Waterworks bathtub is by Herb Ritts.*

ABOVE: *The master bedroom is not a large space. The bedspread on the Lawrence-Bullard-designed bed is made from antique sari fabric. The eye-catching photograph is by Herb Ritts.*
RIGHT: *Lawrence-Bullard also designed the bed and star picture frames in this guesthouse bedroom. Colorful antique textiles complete the exotic mood.*
FOLLOWING PAGES: *For this corner of the large garden that surrounds Cortazzo's country property, Lawrence-Bullard designed outdoor furniture in new weatherproof fabric from Perennials Outdoor Fabrics that looks like it belongs indoors. It gives the space an "Alice-in-Wonderland" effect.*

COSMOPOLITAN COUNTRY

Juan Montoya's Japanese-inspired Ranch in New York's Hudson River Valley

BORN IN BOGOTÁ, COLOMBIA, the designer Juan Montoya has a rich and prolific life. He studied architecture in Colombia, and earned a degree in environmental design at Parsons The New School of Design in New York. Along the way, he also became an artist and sculptor, and both disciplines inform his design work. His elegant patrician decorating can often be seen in the pages of *Architectural Digest*, but when it comes to his country retreat, the designer turned to a more rustic palette. A true cosmopolitan, Montoya has apartments in Paris, Miami, New York, and Bogotá. When asked how he manages to spend time in all of them, he replies, "I have work everywhere, and it is convenient for everyone if I have a place nearby."

Hidden in the hills of the Hudson River Valley, Montoya's country retreat on 110 acres overlooks his own lake. He discovered the property back in 1981, and over the years has extensively reworked the rather plain original house beyond recognition. Today the sweeping driveway leads up to the main house, past the lake and up to a granite brick courtyard. The guesthouse on the left, added some years ago, sits on top of a stone loggia that serves as a sheltered spot for cars.

Entered from an uphill staircase, the main house has many levels. This highly eclectic personal space reflects Montoya's cosmopolitan lifestyle. He has created a rich rural opulence using an earthy palette of browns, beige, and orange, crisply accented with white. His skill as an architect is revealed by his arrangement of indoor spaces, and the combination of the reed ceilings, sisal carpet, and dark reclaimed wood makes the house feel Asian, despite a very European mix of furniture. Once inside, more steps lead up to Montoya's studio. It is filled by a long broad desk, under a large window that has a ship's captain's view over the landscape. The piles of research materials on every surface reveal the designer's extensive preparation for each of his projects. Redefining the word "busy," Montoya has a new furniture collection for Century, as well as fabric, carpet, and accessories collections for other manufacturers—not to mention design projects that stretch from Mexico to France, San Francisco, and, of course, New York.

On the other side of the house are the bedrooms, which have views up into the hillside, which is scattered with large boulders. On the top floor, the master bedroom fits in an A-framed space and has its own deck overlooking the surrounding forest.

On a lower level, Montoya has fashioned a large living space, punctuated by a tall tropical fig tree that reaches up to a skylight. This is a rich masculine room, where dark furniture echoes the woodwork and overhead beams. A large central stone fireplace anchors the rustic mood. Although the designer's love of books is evident throughout the house, Montoya keeps most of them corralled in a small library at one end of this space. On the ground floor, a stone walled dining room has views through a rustic loggia, next to a busy and much-used kitchen. Here, Montoya's partner, Urban Karlsson, whips up delicious lunches for the couple, who, despite all their travels, manages most weekends to escape to this quiet corner of New York state.

*Juan Montoya based the design of his swimming pool on a floor pattern in a Swedish palace.
A stone courtyard at the far end holds an outdoor fireplace used for cooler evenings.*

ABOVE: On the landing that leads to the bedrooms hangs a striking artwork by Norwegian artist Anne-Karin Furunes.
RIGHT: The main living room is a rich mix of Asian influences with a decidedly masculine note. A small round table for meals sits in the far corner.

In the dining room, Montoya used the stone from the property for the floor. The white walls provide a backdrop for the various sculptural objects lining the sideboard.

ABOVE: *In the guesthouse, a chic sacking pillowcase on a Swedish daybed contributes to the rustic look of the room.*
RIGHT: *Montoya's office affords a commanding view over the property. The desk chair is eighteenth-century English. On the desk, you can see his piles of research materials.*

ABOVE: *The guesthouse was originally planned to be a studio for Montoya, who trained as a sculptor, but the space soon became needed to accommodate guests. African figurines are displayed on a small table in front of the window.*
RIGHT: *In the guesthouse, an open iron four-poster bed is the focus of the room.*

COUNTRY LIVING

James Cramer's 1830s Farmhouse in Maryland

"I DON'T LIKE TO TRAVEL," explains stylist and producer James Cramer. "I am in my own little world here in western Maryland." Cramer was "discovered" by a magazine editor nearly twenty-five years ago and ever since has worked as a stylist and magazine producer, especially for country-style publications, including *Cottage Living*. He found this early nineteenth-century farmhouse while searching for a home in the region, which is a convenient hour away from Washington, D.C. and Baltimore.

"I was looking to live in the country, where I could fix up a house and put in a garden," Cramer adds. There are lots of old log houses in Maryland like this one, disguised with newer brick fronts and side walls, but when Cramer saw the rear elevation of this farmhouse at the edge of a small village, he realized its true potential. Inside, he discovered a rarity: an almost completely untouched interior, except for a kitchen added in one of the worst periods for kitchen renovation in history—the 1970s. Wall-to-wall carpet stretched across the floor, even into the earlier brick fireplace. Once these were ripped out, Cramer discovered an original wide-plank floor and a period cooking fireplace. Over the unearthed supporting mantelpiece beam, he added a pair of semicircular shutters salvaged from a house in Cape May Beach, Delaware. The fireplace ensemble, visible from the front door, provides a strong focal point.

For its entire history, the farmhouse had been owned by members of the same family, but was finally sold by a nephew in the middle of a divorce. Plenty of the original woodwork, doors, and latches remained when the designer purchased it. He ripped out drywall ceilings and whitewashed the newly exposed antique beams. A veteran antiques hunter, he is always on the hunt for unusual pieces he can use in his work or at home. Cramer has the rare skill of being able to visualize each object as part of a photographic composition. "I always wanted to do window display, and I put everything I find into photo-ready displays—photographers love me, as everything I do is ready for them."

Unconventionally situated in the entrance, the dining room, with its unexpected white plastic Philippe Starck chairs, is center stage for the hospitable stylist. (Many of his friends live either to the north or south, so Cramer's welcoming farmhouse becomes a halfway point for everyone to meet.) This area leads to a cozy living room with a corner fireplace, where a pair of handmade reproduction Windsor chairs give the space an airy look with their unusual fifteen-spindle backs flanking an antique farm table.

Upstairs, he painted the original wood floor of his large studio white, making it seem even bigger. This is where Cramer plans magazine stories and sketches ideas for rooms and gardens. Here, he created a large table out of a slab of wood and galvanized pipe, and added a modern element with a Marais AC stool, designed by Xavier Pauchard in 1934. The designer likes to use a lot of metal to counterbalance the typical "country" look.

When it was built in 1830, the house came with two hundred acres, but in the intervening 178 years the property has dwindled to one acre. This is still plenty of land for this keen gardener, and it is where Cramer can be found during most of the year. "When I go out in my garden and work, I think of ideas," says Cramer. "It's almost like a meditation."

James Cramer uses the formal entry to his farmhouse as a dining room. White accents include modern plastic chairs by French designer Philippe Starck.

*In the living room, a
modern sofa slip-covered
in white linen is paired
with traditional comb-back
Windsor chairs in a clever
mix of new and old.*

ABOVE: *The living room fireplace was painted gray to match the room's woodwork.*
RIGHT: *Upstairs, Cramer has filled a wall with framed pressed leaves and flowers, set off by the brown painted background.*

ABOVE: In the pantry, Cramer cut sheets of galvanized metal as a modern ironic take on conventional curtains.
RIGHT: The original kitchen fireplace was unearthed in the renovation process. Semicircular shutters salvaged from a Delaware house create a strong decorative focal point above the mantelpiece.

RESTORED TO PERFECTION

Carol Bokuniewicz and John Smallwood's
Nineteenth-century Farmhouse in New Preston, Connecticut

RESTORING THEIR OWN HOUSE often recharges decorators and designers, and provides a canvas for them to experiment with ideas that they can then take further with their clients. When publisher John Smallwood and his wife, art director Carol Bokuniewicz, discovered this Litchfield County farmhouse while searching for a weekend house eight years ago, at first they saw only a very big project. "There was a big hole in the roof," explains Smallwood, "and the interiors were essentially open to the elements." Bokuniewicz was such a committed New Yorker that initially she was panicked about the purchase: "Is this my fate, this farmhouse in the middle of nowhere?"

However, after six months, as the restoration started to become more than just hauling away the trash, she discovered that she, too, was hooked along with her husband. Built in 1805, the house was nicely proportioned and structurally sound. Italianate details added in the mid-nineteenth century were still intact, and the farmhouse featured an ornate central spiral staircase, the legacy of a decorator who had once used this house as a weekend country escape.

Keeping the best features of the building, opening up the rooms, and choosing colors were all creative challenges, and the couple got caught up in the process, often doing some of the work themselves. "It was very satisfying, coming up for a weekend and finishing a small part of the restoration," says

Bokuniewicz. They had a standing appointment with their contractor every Saturday morning to discuss progress, although it took a year of meetings before the house even became livable.

Little by little, the experience working on the house started to inform the couple's other activities. John's publishing company, Smallwood & Stewart, came out with the successful *American Farmhouses*, which included early photographs of their house; this was followed by the best-selling *Home Rules*, a decorating book by Oprah Winfrey's design expert, Nate Berkus. Their home also became a testing ground for Bokuniewicz's design ideas, and this shows in her many new directions. She found herself working with her husband on a big program for Benjamin Moore, which includes books and magazines. Inspired by her new part-time country life, Bokuniewicz has also taken on the New York Botanical Gardens as a client, creating the packaging and branding for their licensed products program, which includes everything from home fragrance, china, bedding, and glassware.

The most dramatic change in the house took place in the kitchen, where a rabbit warren of small storerooms was cleared away to make a big open space. Bokuniewicz cut a foam template to take back to New York for the stainless-steel cabinetmakers, because the old house was hard to measure accurately. "We didn't want to over-restore," explains

A sculptural ceramic bowl by Eva Zeisel and a pot by Jonathan Adler join flea market finds on top of a chest in the dining room.

The nineteenth-century staircase was added by a previous owner, who was a decorator. The striking antique side table was bought at the Brimfield flea market. The walls are painted in Benjamin Moore's Linen White.

Smallwood. "We wanted modern, but to retain the personality of what we had." Of course color can do a lot, and the palette of bright green, browns, and dark grays they chose also makes the old house feel more contemporary. Smallwood loves the local flea markets, and his finds are slowly growing. A delicate stylistic balance has been reached between old and new, which is absorbed into the mix of the house.

Outside, Smallwood spends much of his time in the surrounding nine-acre garden, where there is always a new challenge. "I always wanted a garden," he says. "Besides, it is much easier to entertain outdoors in the summer. Space is too tight in the city." After eight or so years, Bokuniewicz is most surprised by the area's constant social life. Far from being "trapped" in the country as she had first feared, they have made lots of friends here, since Litchfield County is famous for its creative mix of part-time and permanent residents. "We live near fashion designers, decorators, architects, and magazine editors," she says. "We have as busy a social life as in New York."

The vases on the mantelpiece were spray-painted matte black by Smallwood, and the Lucite coffee table was bought at Conran in New York. The sofas are covered in painters' canvas drop cloths for durability.

ABOVE: The couple stained the dining table white and added black Chinese Chippendale-style chairs, bought in Sag Harbor. The white chandelier on top was purchased from decorator Florence de Dampierre. A bright green wall works as an accent to the room.
RIGHT: The imposing mirror leaning against the wall in the living room came from Michael Trapp, while the corner lamp was discovered at the Brimfield flea market. The statue on the pedestal is a reproduction from the Metropolitan Museum of Art in New York.

170 ROOMS TO INSPIRE IN THE COUNTRY

RIGHT: A nineteenth-century French gilded sofa sits at one end of the dining room, flanked by a pair of white plastic Philippe Starck chairs and Giacometti-style standing lamps. Zar, a white wood stain, is used throughout on the floors.
FOLLOWING PAGES: A nineteenth-century wood table unexpectedly paired with blue Arne Jacobson dining chairs provides an informal dining area in the kitchen.

PREVIOUS PAGES: *Carol Bokuniewicz designed the stainless-steel kitchen cabinets and had them manufactured in New York. A George Nelson clock lends a note of punctuation above the stove.*
ABOVE: *The upstairs master bedroom occupies a sunny corner of the house. The couple designed and painted the screens standing in the corners of the room, made from hollow-core doors bought at Home Depot.*
RIGHT: *Dark brown walls give the guest bedroom a relaxing and peaceful ambience. Matching bedside lamps balance the room. Smallwood used a cement grinder on the floor, then gave it several coats of polyurethane.*

SHIP AHOY!

Steven Gambrel's Eighteenth-century Compound in Sag Harbor, New York

DECORATOR STEVEN GAMBREL and his partner Chris Conner discovered Sag Harbor thirteen years ago when they rented a house here with a friend. "It was a decrepit old town down on its luck," explains Gambrel, who is tall and lanky, with a passing resemblance to the actor Jimmy Stewart. They bought a small house and fixed it up, becoming experts in historic preservation in the process, then sold it and bought another. This house was closer to the water but overlooked an abandoned property, which eventually came on the market.

When they saw the historical records, they discovered that this new house was once a much less tranquil property, as the Long Island Rail Road used to thunder past the back door around the edge of the bay. However, in a seemingly arbitrary planning decision the rail line was shut down, and the previous owners got a chance to buy the land, which enlarged the property to more than an acre and gave it direct access to the water. Today, the house has an uninterrupted view of Sag Harbor Cove.

What makes this property so special is that it feels like a mini estate, unusual for a small town like Sag Harbor, whose charm is based on rows of small half houses, some dating as far back as the eighteenth century. These sailors' cottages were built on compact plots of land, with only one front window and a main door to one side. Gambrel's house, erected in 1790, began as a half house but was gradually enlarged over the years, especially in 1967, when it fell victim to a series of botched home-handyman projects. Gambrel and Connor's main focus was to rework the extensions into a comfortable living space while restoring the period core.

For almost a year Conner stationed himself in the guesthouse to supervise construction. This was not a big sacrifice, since the small but charming structure sits on the edge of the water and has the best view of the property. He enjoyed the experience so much that when it was over, "it was hard to move back into the main house," he recalls.

An accomplished New York decorator, one of Gambrel's main strengths is his sophisticated and subtle use of color. In this house for himself, however, he concentrated more on textured surfaces and the reflective quality of glass. "It's nice to have moments where there is almost no color," explains the designer, referring to the work of Belgian designer Axel Vervoordt. "I like his use of texture instead of color." The house seamlessly incorporates layers of Gambrel's collections, found in his travels all over the world, which he layers into an overall beachside theme, using objects with nautical references as well as pewter and glass.

The main house is entered almost directly from the street. Inside, Gambrel put one of his favorite pieces of furniture: a Danish Baroque chest of drawers found in Belgium, topped with a collection of tobacco containers in various types of stone. The eye is led directly through an enfilade of rooms to

The gorgeous Danish Baroque chest of drawers that stands in the entry was found in Belgium. Gambrel topped it with an ornate white Italian ceramic lamp and a collection of stone tobacco boxes.

ABOVE: The 1790 core of the house, which sits peacefully on a quiet street leading from the historic center of Sag Harbor, is masked by various additions over the years.
RIGHT: The one-bedroom guesthouse was extensively reworked. It has the best view of the cove at the end of the garden.

windows that glimpse the sea beyond a broad green lawn. To the left of the entry, one of the oldest rooms in the house has been given a bracing dose of purple, and with a sure hand the designer has combined old and new furniture with meticulous attention to shape and color. A modern sofa upholstered in purple linen, sitting below an abstract sailing painting, works perfectly with the period furniture in this paneled room.

Beyond the spacious pastel-colored dining room, hung in each corner with impressively large brass lamps from Holland, Gambrel added a large kitchen with a view of the cove, incorporating both new and recycled materials. The white marble floor here was rescued from a renovation of the Museum of Modern Art in New York.

The spacious living room leading from the kitchen was once the garage. "Steven and his father shellacked the room in three days," explains Conner, "The eighteenth-century beams in the ceiling are old floor joists discovered in Connecticut." Hanging above the reclaimed fireplace is a zodiac tabletop, once used every day by a fortune-teller in Long Beach, California. They installed large period-style twelve-over-twelve windows along the side that faces the sea, using standard Brosco windows. Their aluminum sides were removed, and the hanging mechanisms were replaced with more traditional chains. Upstairs, Gambrel added an extra wing of bedrooms for visiting friends, which blends well with the rest of the house, as he believes in keeping it stylistically intact. The master bedroom has a commanding view of the water. Above the bed, a large painting by New York contemporary artist Matthew Benedict acts as an extra headboard. "We had to add elements rather than restore the house," Gambrel notes, but the overall impression is of an elegant unity.

A fire burns in one of the original rooms at the front of the main house. Gambrel has introduced a striking color scheme of purple and black. A purple horsehair Bergamo fabric was used on the ottoman.

ABOVE: In the guesthouse, a fish trophy on the wall reinforces the nautical theme. Its large scale adds drama to the small living room. The stairs lead up to a small attic space. RIGHT: The 1940s demilune table against the wall of the breakfast room is by Jean-Michel Frank, originally made for the Indian consulate in Brussels. The table is eighteenth-century Belgian, while the rush chairs are from France.

ABOVE: A corner of the main sitting room, showing Gambrel's subtle use of color.
RIGHT: The reclaimed eighteenth-century beams in the living room were once floor joists in a Connecticut property. Above the fireplace hangs an unusual zodiac tabletop, once used every day by a fortune-teller in California.

Gambrel crafted the kitchen
in the spirit of the rest
of the house. The floor is
laid with reclaimed marble
from the Museum of
Modern Art in New York.
Found at Rejuvenation
Hardware, the light bulbs
are replicas of an 1890
Thomas Edison invention.

ABOVE: An upstairs bedroom is painted Gambrel's favorite shade of blue. A 1950s fish painting adds to the seaside ambience of the room.
RIGHT: Gambrel is skilled in his arrangements of shapes and textures. This outdoor side table near the pool has a gnarled wood base, with an arrangement of plant pots, a glass-based lamp, and nautical weights displayed on top.

ABOVE: *A skillfully added staircase leads from the breakfast room to the master bedroom.*
LEFT: *A detail of the coiled rope, which functions as the handrail for the steep steps.*

LEFT: A pink guest bedroom is decorated with framed images of yachts and rope, cleverly made of fragments from a wallpaper screen.
ABOVE: In the same room, a four-poster bed that Gambrel inherited from his family faces a French camelback sofa.

ABOVE: *Glimpsed down the hallway, the headboard in this added upstairs bedroom is Gambrel's own design.*
RIGHT: *A large painting by New York artist Matthew Benedict hangs over the master bed, which has a view across the garden to the water. A tufted leather bench anchors the end of the bed.*

BEACH MODERN

Molly Duffy and Hugh Burns's Beach Getaway in Southampton, New York

YOU MIGHT EXPECT THIS pretty shingled beach house in Southampton to be very predictably decorated, all neat and trim. But banker Molly Duffy, and her husband, Hugh Burns, who is involved in a financial PR company, knew that their favorite designer, Muriel Brandolini, would give it the fresh chic look that they were after. Inside, the two-story cottage from 1910 is a sophisticated pastel surprise, as Brandolini is known for her skillful use of lush, rich colors.

Waving a magic wand, Brandolini introduced a modern interior without taking away the period charm of the house, and washed the rooms with the palest of pastel colors that make it seem cool even on the hottest summer days. The long, icy blue ground-floor living room runs the width of the house. This potentially awkward space is bisected by sectional seating designed by Pierre Charpin, each piece a different shade of pale green or blue, rather like a pastel sushi cut-roll, to create two seating groups within the room. They are balanced by a pair of Mattia Bonetti *Smarties*, lacquered fiberglass coffee tables, on each side. Above hangs a pair of *Cherry Blossom* chandeliers by Claire Cormier-Fauvel, a talented French artist who has worked for Baccarat. They add a refreshing note of pink. A large Viento carpet from Fedora Design anchors the space. Under the window facing the street, she placed a large custom sofa, upholstered in her own fabric, on an open base, which makes an excellent storage space for books and magazines. The sofa is flanked by a pair of Jonathan Adler lamps, with the addition of pretty embroidered shades of Brandolini's own design.

Brandolini designs in a diverse and eclectic style, but makes the mix coherent with balance and proportion. Her rooms usually explode with ideas, but on closer inspection you will notice the matching lamps and chairs that balance each space. Then she adds strong sculptural accents, like the fire screen in the living room, also by Cormier-Fauvel. Brandolini also has hidden the clumsy heating elements by sheathing them in aluminum boxes fitted neatly under each window.

In the TV room next door, Brandolini used another Pierre Charpin sofa, whose moveable elements can be changed around as needed. Here, she has kept to her cool by-the-seaside palette but added drama with a dynamic dark blue Girasol rug from Fedora. This room leads to a bright airy kitchen hung with white lanterns. A glass-topped dining table sits at one end, positioned for a view of the small back garden and swimming pool. Upstairs, the stairwell is hung with nine embroidered lamps, no two alike, which give the minty green space a sense of fantasy. These "in between" areas are often the hardest to decorate, but Brandolini invariably pulls them off with great élan.

She designed a dramatic yellow and blue abstract bookcase that dominates the study upstairs. Glossy white floors flow throughout the house, uniting the rooms that give it a fresh seaside feel.

"We've rented different beach houses all over Long Island," explains Burns, "and when we started looking to buy, this was our favorite house. We wanted a beach atmosphere, a summery kind of house." Brandolini was so successful that they are keen to come most weekends, including in the middle of winter. "Even then, we always walk on the beach almost every day—you see no one!" laughs Duffy.

RIGHT: A Mattia Bonetti Smarties *coffee table defines one of the two seating groups in the living room. Above it hangs one of a pair of* Cherry Blossom *chandeliers by Claire Cormier-Fauvel who also designed the bold fire screen. FOLLOWING PAGES: The living room is bisected by a sectional seating group by Pierre Charpin in varying cool pastels. Muriel Brandolini designed the built-in window sofa and upholstered it with her own fabric.*

LEFT: *Brandolini designed the elegant bookcase in the living room and boxed in the heating elements with aluminium covers.*
ABOVE: *In the TV room, another segmented Pierre Charpin sofa can be moved or rearranged to create various seating arrangements as needed. Brandolini has kept to the cool seaside colors and added a dramatic Girasol rug.*

ABOVE: In the upstairs study, a D.L. desk by Martin Szekely sits next to a dramatic Brandolini-designed bookcase. The rug is by Fedora design.
RIGHT: A detail of the impressively clever blue and green bookcase.

The open kitchen and dining area looks out to the swimming pool. The glossy white floors run through every room and give the house a country feel. White blinds shield against the summer sun.

The stairwell is decorated with nine embroidered lamps of different shapes and hung at different heights. Not one is the same, and they give the minty green space a sense of whimsy.

HAPPY CHIC

Simon Doonan and Jonathan Adler's Weekender in Shelter Island, New York

"I AM CONVINCED THAT THE KEY to our happiness might well be found in our decor," writes Simon Doonan, a regular columnist for the *New York Observer*. A visit to the Shelter Island beach house that he shares with his partner, designer and potter Jonathan Adler, confirms that only truly happy people could live here. Nothing dull about this A-frame building, built in 1972 by a Pan Am pilot—it brims with 1970s optimism and joie de vivre. The walls are painted white, as a foil for the couple's exuberant self-expression, and it is filled to the brim with Adler designs: pottery, rugs, and artwork, even prototypes for bud vases and towels. Doonan tends to keep a watchful eye on what arrives, as it could easily get out of hand—Adler produces an enormous range of products for his eight home-design stores around the country.

This was not always the case. When the couple bought the house ten years ago, it was Doonan's window-dressing skills that fueled the renovations. As creative director of Barney's New York, he is famous for designing their store windows, which are as much about social commentary as display. Gradually, as Adler's enthusiasm moved from his first love, pottery, into further aspects of home design, he started to take more of an interest. Although Doonan concedes "we've done everything backwards"—having moved the deck three times over the years, for example—they are now happy with the house and are working together on the tropically inspired landscaping.

This compact, modern beach house opens right into a double-height living room, creating an impression of generous space. Leading off the kitchen, which is the center of the house, is a master bedroom that was added quite soon after the couple moved in. A row of high windows gives privacy as well as views of the sky at night. Stumbling visitors heading upstairs to the mezzanine with suitcase in hand know they have arrived at their destination when they see a bed with a huge graphic "GUEST" on the bedspread.

Sunset magazine, a San Francisco-based publication that produced iconic design and landscaping books in the 1950s and '60s, has been a great resource to the designers. "They had the sunny optimism of the California lifestyle, a kind of rustic modernism that appealed to us," explains Doonan, "a pre-Ralph Lauren kind of vision."

The couple drives out from Manhattan most weekends, even in the winter. Here, next to the beach, Doonan finds time for his column and other writings. He is the co-author of at least four books, and the author of three more, including the hilarious autobiography *Confessions of a Window Dresser* and *Nasty: My Family and Other Glamorous Varmints*, which has been optioned by the BBC for a TV series. Doonan's latest is *Eccentric Glamour: Creating an Insanely More Fabulous You*. We all need this book.

Adler has his own best seller, *My Prescription for Anti-Depressive Living*, which expounds on the design philosophy behind this house and the other two places the couple owns in New York and Miami Beach. His fundamental philosophy is to decorate with color, wit, and humor. Appropriately enough, his next project is a hotel in Las Vegas.

An eclectic and colorful selection of summer hats stands right by the front door.

ABOVE: The main living room has a colorful furniture palette—even though the walls themselves have been painted white. A hanging basket chair provides the perfect nook from which to watch television. RIGHT: The orange front door opens directly onto the living room, which like most of the house is furnished with a collection of thrift-store finds and Jonathan Adler prototypes.

ABOVE: Even the most jet-lagged guest couldn't miss the upstairs spare bedroom.
RIGHT: An eclectic collection of oversize keys hang above a bright purple desk upstairs. On the left sits a small Adler-designed lamp.

ABOVE: The master bedroom was added by the couple to enlarge their relatively small beach house. A shelf running along the top of the windows is the perfect place to display a collection of Adler objects and vintage pots. *RIGHT:* Inspired by old Sunset magazines, Doonan and Adler added a swimming pool to the stretch of land behind their house. Sturdy bamboo gives the garden a Californian vibe.

PART IV
COUNTRY GARDEN DESIGN

OUTDOOR "ROOMS"

WE OWE THE WORD "PARADISE" to the ancient Persians. Although they did not have country gardens as we know them, *pairidaeza* means "enclosure" or "park," and represented the creation of a perfect outdoor space. A well-designed enclosed garden space full of scented flowers and leafy greenery provided a peaceful place to relax, to read a book, or to listen to the gentle sound of water splashing in a nearby fountain—a true paradise.

For a country house, there are endless opportunities to create these kinds of outdoor "rooms" or enclosed garden spaces. Here you do not have the space limitations of a suburban backyard—only your time and imagination set the boundaries. An outdoor room may be as simple as a few chairs and a patch of gravel, perhaps a carefully defined bordered terrace, or a vast landscape of pagodas and cactus, like Tony Duquette's fantasy garden in the hills of Malibu.

A sense of enclosure helps give the outdoor garden a peaceful feeling of sanctuary. There are many ways of achieving this. An existing wall can be pressed into service, or a new one built to surround the space. Planting a hedge on at least two sides creates a natural, organic screen: evergreen is ideal for this in northern climates, as it provides structure to the garden year-round. A planted square of trees can also define a room. Large flowering bushes, such as azaleas or hydrangeas, have the benefit of providing a colorful backdrop to outdoor meals: they can be chosen to add an extra element of fragrance to the summer garden. A canopy of trees, such as ficus, not only provides shade and shelter, but also creates a dramatic natural roof. Sheltered porches and verandas are perfect places to move into once winter is over and the warm weather arrives. Here, you have the luxury of adding sofas and armchairs, even paintings and mirrors, since they are protected from the wind and rain.

Garden furniture should be well designed, solid, durable, and in the same style, color, and material, since too many alternating sizes and shapes distract from the beauty of the surroundings. A permanent bench, painted a harmonious green or silvery gray and set in a place for quiet contemplation, is the perfect choice for a country garden seat.

PREVIOUS PAGES: In the Santa Barbara countryside, a simple circle of Adirondack chairs functions as an outdoor room.
RIGHT: Designer Linda Garland added a spectacular combination bridge/living room across a small river on her estate, Panchoran, in Bali.

CLOCKWISE FROM TOP LEFT: *Artist James Brown and his wife Alexandra furnished this Mexican veranda for outdoor lunches with their children. An Australian country porch has a comfortable wicker chair perfect for contemplating the view, shared by a farm cat. Overlooking the Connecticut hills, Michael Trapp's deck is an extension of his house. In this outdoor living room, he can host large dinner parties or relax with friends. A hedge can function as a wall to define an outdoor room. This living space in California has a carefully thought-out color combination of greens and yellows. A conveniently placed bench by a garden wall creates another small outdoor "room."*

CLOCKWISE FROM TOP LEFT: *A Californian palm tree provides enough shade for this attractive year-round seating landscaped with potted succulents. Designer Kate Stamps lives in a country-like estate in South Pasadena, where she has added an arbor to her rose garden to frame a comfortable bench. Outdoor walls can be enlivened by more than just paint. Here, an attractive tile panel brings interest to this "room."*

CLOCKWISE FROM TOP LEFT: *A furnished veranda in Jamaica affords a beautiful place to have breakfast and watch the morning mist rise. Decorator Tom Fallon lives on his Shelter Island porch in the summer. His comfortable green-painted wicker furniture is sturdy and will last for many generations of family summers. This outdoor room has been created with gravel and plants. The blue garden furniture transports this Californian garden to France. The author's front porch becomes an extension of the living room in the summer. Metal plates decorating the wall give it an indoor feel. The floor rug was bought at Target.*

CLOCKWISE FROM TOP LEFT: *Chris Cortazzo's pool house has been created by decorator Martyn Lawrence-Bullard to function as a comfortable living room. Hidden above the cupboards against the far wall is a flat-screen TV. The fireplace makes it a cozy spot in the cool Californian evenings. Lawrence-Bullard treated the entire stretch of lawn at Cortazzo's house as an outdoor room, even designing a Victorian-style "conversational" round sofa, covered in outdoor fabrics. In the same garden, wing chairs lend formality to this dining arrangement overlooking a stream. Large outdoor lanterns on the table add to the natural grandeur of the decorating scheme. Muriel Brandolini lunches almost every day on the lawn of her Hampton Bays house. A table covered in a colorful cloth and a row of chairs produce an instant dining room.*

WATER ELEMENTS AND SWIMMING POOLS

ONCE REGARDED AS ONE of the four basic elements of the universe, water has great symbolic value. The sight of fountains, ponds, rivers, and pools has always lifted the spirits. There are many ways to include it as part of the garden. For example, use long thin troughs of water to link architectural elements in the landscape, as seen all over the Middle East; or be inspired by eighteenth-century France and shoot water through nozzles to create airy compositions in geometric patterns and designs.

A symbol of life and prosperity, fountains in dry climates emphasize the luxury of water. They come in all shapes and sizes, and can be tiled or in a variety of stone. A fountain not only provides a destination in the garden, but also can add a strong focal point to the front entrance of a house. Another dramatic water element in a country garden is a large, reflecting lake, which magnifies and doubles the surrounding view. Although needing careful planning, it is worth it—in the right location, a lake can transform a country property. On a smaller scale, a pond has the same appeal, although its borders should look completely natural.

A swimming pool can either be a formal decorative feature, or create a resortlike atmosphere to the house, making you feel as if you are always on vacation. Essentially a twentieth-century addition to the garden, swimming pools were first designed like the ornamental ponds that preceded them. Care should be taken so that it doesn't become a harsh element in the landscape. The ideal spot should be relatively flat and easily accessible—keep an open mind when deciding, and remember that outbuildings and trees can be moved. Placed in front of the house, perhaps with a facing pool house or gazebo, a pool lends a touch of classical elegance to the landscape.

Today most local building codes require pools to be protected from wandering children and nonswimmers. This means that it is often practical to locate the pool close to the house and utilize preexisting boundaries. Fencing can be disguised as hedges, and walls can be hidden with bushes; one of the most successful boundaries I have seen is a New England-style natural stone wall laid without grout, with the same stone used as decking around the pool. The larger the fenced space, the better.

Most people spend a great deal of time looking at their pool rather than swimming in it. Choose a design that is in keeping with the architectural style of the main house and select the same or complementary materials, colors, and shapes. Rectangular or square pools are the most popular shapes; the "freeform" pool has gone the way of the 1960s and looks awkward today. Softer shades of blue or green help blend a pool into a garden, and many people find this approach more natural with a rural backdrop. Too much hardscaping is often unnecessary. Defining boundaries with plants, hedges, and lawns, which can be planted right up to the pool edge, is the one of the best ways to achieve a more natural look. Garden elements like urns or large pots can define the corners of the pool and give it more structure.

Rose Tarlow's timeless swimming pool in her California garden is an excellent example of a natural-looking pool that sits in harmony with the landscape.

CLOCKWISE FROM TOP LEFT: *Architect Steven Ehrlich designed this Californian pool, which is screened by soft bamboo plantings. Architect Manolo Mestre created this Jacuzzi-with-a-view on the side of a hill in Valle de Bravo, Mexico. A fountain and rill give structure to this Santa Barbara garden.*

CLOCKWISE FROM TOP LEFT: *Coordinated pool furniture, designed by Tom Beeton, defines a small pool in California. Designers Andrew Fisher and Jeffery Wiseman thought carefully about placement when they built their Napa Valley swimming pool. Its elegant proportions are defined by shell-encrusted lighting and a row of seating. This pool has been lined with rocks to give a natural look to the garden. In Virginia, artist and designer Dana Westring added interest to his pool with this antique spout.*

CLOCKWISE FROM TOP LEFT: Brian Tichenor and Raun Thorp are a skilled husband-and-wife architectural team. For their Southern California pool, they included a gazebo for summer entertaining that stretches the width of the pool. Steven Gambrel added a pool and pavilion to a Sag Harbor garden. Notice the elegant simplicity of the structure and pool proportions. Westring's pool in Virginia is surrounded by discreet fencing. A shady gazebo shelters outdoor furniture for casual meals. Linda Garland designed an outdoor bathroom shower—perfect for the mild tropical climate of her Balinese country estate—and added water-loving plants on tall sponges. Achva Stein landscaped this dramatic Smith-Miller and Hawkinson pool on a film producer's California property.

CLOCKWISE FROM TOP LEFT: *A beautiful view in Mexico is made more enjoyable by clever placement of a deck for dining over the swimming pool designed by architect Manolo Mestre. Martyn Lawrence-Bullard added a row of potted shrubs to define a Malibu swimming pool. Another view of the Westring pool shows how to overcome the disadvantages of a sloping ground. The retaining walls are softened by skillful plantings. Decorator Robert Couturier designed this French-style water feature in Mexico.*

GARDEN STRUCTURES

CLASSIC EIGHTEENTH-CENTURY English gardens and parks were punctuated with follies, pagodas, and other fanciful garden structures. Inspired by a visit in 1786 to the great English landscape park Stowe, Thomas Jefferson planned four different pavilions for his garden at Monticello, each in a different architectural style of architecture—Gothic, Neoclassical, Chinese, and French.

With today's emphasis on outdoor living, pavilions are still a civilized way to add living space to a country home. A pagoda or roofed gazebo, built where there is a view, can be one of the nicest ways to enjoy a garden. It is a year-round outdoor room in some parts of this country. Because it is protected from the elements, dining chairs and tables can be kept here without the need to store them in bad weather. Placed strategically at the end of a pool, a gazebo is a comfortable spot to relax or read a book.

A freestanding arbor is another useful way to provide a shaded seating area. It can serve as a natural link for various parts of the garden and creates a structural composition during the barren winter. Providing storage is important, too. Small out buildings are a good solution as they can hold both extra outdoor furniture and garden tools.

As with all elements to the garden, style is important. There has to be a visual link between the design of the structures and that of the main house or swimming pool. A round ornamental gazebo complements a Victorian house, for example, while a single cubelike structure will match a modernist building to perfection. Harmony of architectural styles keeps a rural property looking appropriate in the surrounding landscape.

Sadly, there are few attractive prefabricated garden structures. The proportions are usually clumsy and the materials not strong enough to stand the test of time. This is one part of the garden where it pays to bring in an architect or designer who can draw up something unique and pleasing.

RIGHT: This small Connecticut outhouse was part of the original property that Dr. Howard and Fran Kiernan bought several years ago from their friends Fritz and Dana Rohn. FOLLOWING PAGES: Designer Tony Duquette spent most of his free time building pagodas on his country property in Malibu. This one resembled a large birdcage, and was put together with various antique elements and given a unifying spray of his favorite color green.

CLOCKWISE FROM TOP LEFT: *A useful toolshed at the back of Jeffrey Morgan's country garden in Kent, Connecticut. Westring built this picturesque building in his Virginia garden. White roses are trained to grow over a small Californian greenhouse. Jock and Ally Spivy use this small old garage to store garden equipment and bicycles at their Kinderhook country house. A garden archway is given more importance when cleverly designed. A small outdoor building like this one can become a retreat from the world.*

GARDEN ELEMENTS

EVERY GARDEN NEEDS A FOCUS. Whether you are starting from scratch with property that stretches out like a large blank canvas, or simply maintaining one that is long established with stately trees and well-cared-for plants, a garden comes alive with the clear hand of a designer and a thoughtfully defined plan. There are many elements to consider, from the practical to the purely decorative: a path to a natural or introduced feature, like a statue or gazebo, stairs to link different levels, or an arched walkway, for example. A path or walkway is a good way to feature plants, which can be placed to their best advantage on either side; imagine an allée of waist-high lavender or irises. Gates, stairways, and pergolas add visual interest and are great for supporting hearty flowering vines and decorative plants, like a climbing rose.

Traditionally gardens incorporated decorative objects like sundials, figures, obelisks, urns, and vases. Care must be taken to place them at natural observation spots, because if they are scattered without consideration, they become distracting. A statue of Buddha at the end of a vista becomes a moment for contemplation, but it loses its meaning if placed randomly by the side of a path. The background for these decorative elements should be kept simple; a plain wall or a leafy green hedge works best, so that the ornament, or statue, is the center of attention.

Besides serving the practical purposes of keeping your feet dry and providing a level place to walk, pathways give structure to a garden. They also act as a background for plants, and perhaps a base for fragrant herbs like mint and thyme, which can be planted in the crevices. In a rural landscape, natural stone, gravel, or aged brick have an appropriate organic look. There is nothing worse than harsh concrete walkways slicing into the lawn to make even the most rustic property look like a municipal park. Stone is one of the most versatile landscape building materials available. It is important to keep your choices simple, however, as too many abrupt changes in the path covering are unattractive and can be visually confusing. Transitions should be carefully thought out. Gravel is one material that can bridge another; it can lead directly and gracefully onto the lawn or a paved stone or brick area without being disruptive.

For those who live in seasonal climates, keep in mind that garden elements are often the most dominant feature of the landscape in winter, so their relationship in a bare garden should be carefully thought out. A property entrance should be planned to look good year-round, with elements like gates and finials surrounded by evergreen trees and shrubs. A garden can be enjoyed even in winter, when the sun creates summer-like conditions, and a seating group in a warm corner is one of the nicest places to spend a few hours with a good book.

Designers Jorge Almada and Anne-Marie Midy introduced an extra formality to their Mexican courtyard garden by adding a Neoclassical-style terra-cotta urn.

CLOCKWISE FROM TOP LEFT: *Designer Ron Mann created a simple branch sculpture to mark the dividing line between his garden in Northern California and the surrounding countryside. Stairs provide a change of level in Westring's Virginia garden. Fritz and Dana Rohn added a graceful statue as the centerpiece of their country garden in Connecticut. The sympathetic use of old stone for both the pathway and the walls lends character to Michael Trapp's garden in rural Connecticut. Designer Kate Stamps employed an obelisk to mark a turning point in her South Pasadena garden. To provide definition, Trapp added found architectural objects to a small pond in the back garden of his Connecticut store.*

ABOVE: An arbor adds poetry and romance to Westring's garden in Virginia.
RIGHT: The simple elegance of this urn on its gracious plinth needs no more background than an plain ficus hedge.

DESIGNER DIRECTORY

The following architects, interior designers, designers, and antiques dealers have homes or design projects featured in this book, and several have their own furnishing lines and shops. Also included are the locations of featured house museums.

Jonathan Adler
Jonathan Adler Interior Design
212-645-2802
www.jonathanadler.com
For interior design projects, contact
id@jonathanadler.com

BAMO
510 Third Street
San Francisco, California 94107
415-979-9880
www.bamo.com

Beauport
A National Historic Landmark
The Sleeper-McCann House
75 Eastern Point Boulevard
Gloucester, Massachusetts 01930
978-283-0800
Beauport@HistoricNewEngland.org
www.historicnewengland.org

Muriel Brandolini
525 East 72nd Street
New York, New York 10021
212-249-4920
www.murielbrandolini.com

Jorge Almada and
Anne-Marie Midy
Casamidy
Hospicio 2
San Miguel de Allende,
Guanajuato 37700
Mexico
casamidy@casamidy.com

Robert Couturier
69 Mercer Street
New York, New York 10012
212-463-7177
robert@robertcouturier.com
www.robertcouturier.com

Tony Duquette, Inc.
Hutton Wilkinson, President
P.O. Box 69858
West Hollywood, California 90069
310-271-4688
www.tonyduquette.com

Tom Fallon
100 Riverside Drive, Suite 16B
New York, New York 10024
212-579-6064
tom@tomfallondesign.com
www.tomfallondesign.com

Steven Gambrel
S. r. Gambrel Inc.
270 Lafayette Street, Suite 805
New York, New York 10012
212-925-3380
www.srgambrel.com

Linda Garland
www.lindagarland.com

Jaya Ibrahim
Jaya International Design
5875 Collins Avenue
Miami Beach, Florida 33140
305-868-0081
www.jayainternational.com

Jock and Ally Spivy chose American Gothic chairs in their Kinderhook house for their exotic shapes.
RIGHT: A colorful bedroom in Muriel Brandolini's Hampton Bays beach house. Two pink Chinese Chippendale-style chairs flank the four-poster bed.

Jennings and Rohn Antiques
289 Main Street South
Woodbury, Connecticut 06798
203-263-3775
jennings.rohn@sbcglobal.net
www.jenningsandrohnantiques.com

Martyn Lawrence-Bullard
Martyn Lawrence-Bullard Design
8101 Melrose Avenue
Los Angeles, California 90046
323-655-5080
info@martynlawrencebullard.com
www.martynlawrencebullard.com

Architect Manolo Mestre
Reforma 2009
Lomas, Mexico City, Distrito Federal
11000
Mexico
52-155-5596-0412

Juan Montoya
330 East 59th Street
New York, New York 10022
212-421-2400
info@juanmontoyadesign.com
www.juanmontoyadesign.com

Jeffrey Morgan
Historic Consultant
82 Davis Road
South Kent, Connecticut 06785
doctordust82@yahoo.com

Poke Gardens
Dana Scott Westring Studio
3284 Whiting Road
Marshall, Virginia 20115
540-270-3591
DanaWestring@pokeGardens.com
www.pokegardens.com

Olana State Historic Site
5720 State Route 9G
Hudson, New York 12534
518-828-0135
www.olana.org

Tony Sparks Carpentry
Bantam, Connecticut 06750
860-480-0756

Kate Stamps
318 Fairview Avenue
South Pasadena, California 91030
626-441-5600
www.stampsandstamps.com

Tim Street-Porter Photography
323-549-0122
www.timstreet-porter.com

Rose Tarlow-Melrose House
8454 Melrose Place
Los Angeles, California 90069
323-651-2202
www.rosetarlow.com

Tichenor & Thorp Architects
8730 Wilshire Boulevard
Penthouse 2
Beverly Hills, California 90211
310-358-8444

Michael Trapp
7 River Road
West Cornwall, Connecticut 06796
860-672-6098
www.michaeltrapp.com

Ellen Ward Scarborough Antiques
Overbrook Farm
356 Riverbank Road
Stamford, Connecticut 06903
203-329-0100
wardltd@aol.com
www.ellenwardscarboroughantiques.com